Murder & Crime

LAKE DISTRICT

Murder & Crime
LAKE DISTRICT

MARTIN BAGGOLEY

The
History
Press

This book is for Gillian, David, Rosalie and Peter

First published 2010

The History Press
The Mill, Brimscombe Port
Stroud, Gloucestershire, GL5 2QG
www.thehistorypress.co.uk

British Library Cataloguing in Publication Data.
A catalogue record for this book is available from the British Library.

ISBN 978 0 7524 4805 3

Typesetting and origination by The History Press
Printed in India by Aegean Offset Printers, New Delhi

CONTENTS

ACKNOWLEDGEMENTS

I am grateful to the staff at Barrow and Carlisle Libraries, the staff at the British Newspaper Library at Colindale, and to Enid Hunt for their help.

ONE

THE BEAUTY OF BUTTERMERE AND THE GREAT IMPOSTOR

⚜ KESWICK, 1802 ⚜

In 1792, John Palmer's book, *A Fortnight's Ramble in the Lakes in Westmoreland, Lancashire and Cumberland*, was published, which included an account of a visit he made to a desolate inn at Buttermere. It bore no name, and it was in this small out-of-the-way establishment that he met Mary Robinson, the beautiful fifteen-year-old daughter of the innkeeper. The smitten rambler gave a vivid description of her attractive oval face, delicate features, long dark brown hair and blue eyes.

Following the book's publication, Mary's fame spread quickly throughout the country, and she became known as the Beauty of Buttermere. Many visitors came to the inn especially to see her, but she remained the shy and unassuming girl she had always been. In the years that followed she had many suitors, all of whom were rejected; that was until ten years had passed.

In mid-July 1802, a handsome, middle-aged gentleman arrived in Keswick and registered at the Queen's Head Inn. Under the name of Colonel Alexander Augustus Hope, Member of Parliament for Linlithgow, and brother of the Earl of Hopetoun, he arrived in a splendid carriage, but without staff. This was highly unusual for a gentleman of his social standing, and he explained that he had decided to travel alone, after his servants had expressed a great deal of anxiety at the prospect of visiting the mountainous and desolate Lake District.

He impressed his listeners with descriptions of his estates in Herefordshire, at Castle Douglas near Dumfries, and at Stockport in Cheshire. He spoke of his eventful military campaigns, and would show the wounds he received in North America and Egypt. A gentleman of leisure, he particularly enjoyed fishing on Lake Buttermere, and it was whilst on these trips that he would stay at Mr and Mrs Robinson's inn, where he met the now twenty-five-year-old Mary, who had remained as beautiful as ever and was still single.

MARY of BUTTERMERE.

Above: *Lake Buttermere provided the magnificent backdrop to a tale of deceit and betrayal. (Cumbria County Council)*

Left: *Mary was popular with her father's customers. (Author's collection)*

Colonel Hope made it clear to those he met that he did not wish his presence in the neighbourhood to become widely known. This, he insisted, was to avoid publicity, as he hoped for a quiet and restful stay. Nevertheless, this desire for privacy and the continuing absence of servants led to a whispering campaign by those who were suspicious of him. However, he made several influential and wealthy friends, including Joseph Skelton, a local landowner, who accompanied him to an estate that was for sale in the district, which the Colonel said he was interested in buying, and also John Crump, a wealthy and amiable Liverpool merchant, who was enjoying an extended holiday with his family in Keswick.

However, it was with Colonel Nathaniel Moore, former member for Strabane in the late Irish Parliament, with whom he formed an especially close relationship, and the two men spent many hours sharing memories of their respective distinguished military careers. Colonel Moore was acting as guardian to a beautiful young Irish heiress, known at the time simply as Miss D. Colonel Hope courted her, and within a very short time she agreed to marry him. Surprised at this sudden development, Colonel Moore was nevertheless delighted at the news and gave his blessing to their engagement.

Miss D. was eagerly anticipating a large society wedding, to which her beloved's distinguished relatives and friends would be invited, and she was keen that her friends should hear the good news as soon as possible. However, Colonel Hope urged discretion and insisted on keeping the news secret for the time being. As the days passed without an announcement of the wedding being made, Colonel Moore was perplexed, and Miss D. became more insistent that their engagement should be made public. Then, on Friday 1 October, Colonel Moore received a note from his friend saying that he had to make an urgent visit to one of his estates in Scotland and would be away for a few days. The note continued by saying that, given the short notice, he was short of cash, and enclosed was a bill of exchange for £30 drawn on John Crump, promising that the full amount would be paid within ten days. Colonel Moore had no hesitation in sending the £30 to Colonel Hope by messenger.

His friend was indeed planning a trip to Scotland the following day, but not for the reason given in the letter. On 25 September he had travelled to Whitehaven with Revd Nicholson to obtain a licence to marry Mary Robinson. They were married on 2 October at Loweswater by Revd Nicholson, and after the service the couple set off on their honeymoon, intent on touring Scotland. Initially they stayed at Longtown, and on 4 October the vicar received a letter from his friend, franked as usual 'A.A. Hope, Member of Parliament', saying that they were having an enjoyable time and giving the post office at Longtown as a contact address. It is probable that the Colonel had an ulterior motive in encouraging Revd Nicholson to reply, for he was no doubt keen to learn of the response in the district to the news of his marriage to Mary.

A few days earlier, George Wood, who had been a guest at the wedding, returned to Keswick shortly after the ceremony, and stunned everyone with the news. An enraged Colonel Moore could not believe that a gentleman would behave in such an underhand manner, and began to have doubts that the man was who he purported to be. He immediately produced the bill of exchange, which was honoured by the ever-faithful John Crump, who had earlier received a note from Colonel Hope to expect such a demand. However, this failed to placate Colonel Moore, who wrote to the Earl of Hopetoun in an attempt to establish if the man was indeed his brother, as he claimed to be. Revd Nicholson wrote to his friend in Longtown to advise him of the shock with which the news of his marriage to Mary had been greeted, and also of Colonel Moore's concerns. Colonel Hope was quick to respond by sending the following letter, franked with his signature, and thus without the postage having had to be paid:

Sunday night, 10th Oct. 1802

Very Dear and Reverend Sir,

Anxious that my dear Mary might hear from her parents as soon as possible, we returned from Scotland to this town on Friday evening, and shall most probably proceed for Carlisle tomorrow. Indeed, your letter received this afternoon makes me very desirous of returning to Buttermere, that I may properly answer all such persons as assume the privilege of censuring my conduct, and are mean enough to disturb the peace of our parents.

We are, thank God, very well and happy, as our friends can wish us. The Colonel has given himself a great deal of unnecessary trouble, and I am sorry for it; because ere this, he will be sorry too. I wrote to him on Wednesday last, and this day find his handwriting on the superscription of a letter forwarded to me from Keswick. If I had ever expressed to him any affection for Miss D. except such as you have witnessed, if I had ever even dropped a word on the subject to him, he might have had some plea for complaint. But God knows, and he knows, I never did. He has my free leave to proclaim to all the world, if he finds any pleasure in such proceedings, but no person who really knows me will believe that Miss D. has been deceived by me.

I wish I could be certain when this will reach you, but fearing it may not be at Cockermouth soon enough for you to get it by the market people on the morrow, it is not in my power to say when or where we can meet previous to my arrival at Buttermere, which will very probably be before the middle of this week.

Be pleased to present my best respects to Mrs and Miss Wood … I will remember with permanent gratitude their goodness on this occasion; and amidst the strange vicissitudes of this very eventful life, perhaps I may be blessed with some opportunity of showing how truly sensible I am of every kindness done to me on this occasion.

With the truest respect, esteem and gratitude to all my well wishers, I am,

Very Dear and Reverend Sir,

Your ever,

A. HOPE

Love and duty attend those to whom they are due, and I beg you will tell them not to make any preparation for our return, for I shall have to move about almost as soon as I arrive, and Mary will love quietness.

When he and Mary returned home on Tuesday 12 October, there were many questions requiring answers from the Colonel. Details of the marriage had been published across the border in Scotland, where friends of Colonel Hope had been surprised to hear the news, as they believed him to be in Vienna. Reports of their concern soon reached Keswick, and coincidentally, George Harding, a barrister and friend of Colonel Hope, had recently arrived in the town.

Having heard the rumours of an apparent impostor, Mr Harding invited the recently returned honeymooner to meet him for dinner at the Queen's Head, where he was staying.

Keswick. (Cumbria County Council)

At first, Colonel Hope seemed reluctant to accept the invitation but decided to go, and travelled by horse from Buttermere to Keswick. He was met by Mr Wood, who, despite the rumours circulating about his friend, agreed to hand over £30 for a bill of exchange in that amount to be repaid by Mr Crump.

The moment Mr Harding met his guest he denounced him as an impostor, dismissing the man's protestations of innocence, and of being a victim of a series of misunderstandings. Mr Harding persuaded Mr Wood to secure the man's horse to prevent his escape, and to summon the town's constable. Mr Wood did so, but appears to still have had faith in the accused man, for he did not ask for his money to be returned.

The constable was presented with a dilemma. On the one hand there was Mr Harding, a stranger in the district who was making serious accusations; on the other there was the accused, who was protesting his innocence, declaring that there had been a simple misunderstanding, and who was supported by Revd Nicholson. Eventually, the constable agreed to allow the accused man to row across the lake to be with Mary at the inn at Buttermere, in a boat loaned to him by Mr Burkett, a friend with whom he had often fished.

As he rowed away from the little quay, he was waved off by Mr Burkett, Revd Nicholson and a small group of well-wishers. However, he did not arrive at the inn, and Mary would never see him again. Instead, having recognised that he had been exposed for the scoundrel he really was, the impostor made good his escape.

John Hatfield.
(Author's collection)

When it was realised the Colonel had absconded, a local magistrate issued a warrant for his arrest, and ordered that a search be made of his property at the inn, but nothing was found that pointed to his true identity. One of his possessions was an elegant dressing case, which Mary decided to search again. She found a secret drawer, in which she discovered a number of letters. They were addressed to the man in his real name of John Hatfield. To make the discovery even more hurtful to Mary, it became evident to her that the letters had been sent to him by his wife, and they also contained news of their children.

Once his true identity had become known, details of this notorious fraudster's background began to emerge. He was born in Mottram-in-Longdale, Cheshire to his parents William and Betty, and was baptised on 24 May 1759. As a youth he began work as a rider, or commercial traveller, for a linen draper, which entailed extensive travel throughout the north of England. However, it was not long before he embarked on his criminal career.

Shortly after starting work, he learnt of a Cheshire farmer and his wife, with whom he was acquainted, who had recently revealed to their daughter that they were not her natural parents, and that she was the illegitimate daughter of Lord Robert Manners. The couple had been acting as her guardians, but of great interest to the youthful Hatfield was the revelation that His Lordship intended giving her £1,000, on condition she married a man he approved of.

Hatfield lost no time in approaching the farmer, and presented himself as a young man with excellent prospects. He sought permission to marry the young woman, and a meeting was arranged with Lord Robert Manners. It was a successful interview and His Lordship, who was impressed with Hatfield, gave his consent. Indeed, he was so impressed that on the day following the marriage, £1,500 was deposited in Hatfield's bank account.

Hatfield was clearly in an enviable position for such a young man. He was married to a beautiful young woman; he had a job with prospects, and a substantial fortune to his name. However, this was not enough for him, and despite this wonderful start to his adult life, he abandoned his wife and headed for London a few days after receiving the money. Here he followed a feckless and dissolute lifestyle. He spent much of his time in the coffee houses of Covent Garden, boasting of being a relation of the Duke of Rutland, and of his various estates throughout the country.

Nothing further was heard of him for several years, but he seems to have returned to his wife, for by 1782 they were living together with their three children. However, domesticity was not for him, and he again deserted his family. His wife died shortly afterwards, and his children, for whom he showed not the slightest concern, were forced to live on the charity of relatives.

Once more in London, he lived by fraud and deception, regularly passing forged bills of exchange on wealthy individuals, who, after realising they had been duped, were usually too embarrassed to prosecute him. Eventually however, he was held in the King's Bench Prison for an unpaid debt of £160, but this did not prevent him from boasting to the other prisoners of his non-existent property and aristocratic relations.

One of his fellow inmates was Valentine Morris, the disgraced former governor of St Vincent, who in 1779 had negotiated a humiliating surrender of the colony to the French. On his return to England, the hapless diplomat had been thrown into gaol for debt. He was visited regularly by a clergyman who was always prepared to help prisoners in any way he could. Hatfield managed to persuade him that he was a relative of the Duke of Rutland, who did not know of his incarceration. He asked the kindly man of God if he would visit the Duke and explain his predicament.

The meeting with the Duke was hugely embarrassing for the vicar, who was told that Hatfield was not his relation, and that he had never heard of him. The vicar wasted no time in confronting Hatfield and remonstrating with him. Nevertheless, much to Hatfield's delight, the Duke later remembered that the illegitimate daughter of his relative, Lord Robert Manners, had married a tradesman named Hatfield. He sent a messenger to the gaol to make discrete enquiries and upon learning that Hatfield was that man, the Duke paid the debt, and Hatfield was once again free.

In 1784, the Duke of Rutland was appointed Lord Lieutenant of Ireland, and Hatfield decided to follow him to Dublin, where he registered in one of the city's leading hotels. He explained to the manager that he was a kinsman of the Duke, but was unable to visit him at the castle until his own horses, carriage and servants arrived from England. The manager was persuaded to allow him to stay at the hotel without payment until his property and staff arrived.

Hatfield made himself known to the gentlemen of leisure who frequented Dublin's coffee houses, to whom he boasted unashamedly. He spoke of his relationship to the Duke and of his many estates. However, as time passed, the hotel manager became increasingly suspicious of his guest and demanded that the £60 bill should be paid. Of course, Hatfield could not pay it, and he was once again thrown into gaol for debt.

Displaying no sense of shame or embarrassment, Hatfield had no hesitation in writing to the Duke, explaining his unfortunate situation. Keen to avoid the possibility of a scandal if Hatfield remained in the city, the Duke agreed to settle the debt, but this was on condition that he left Ireland. The debt having been paid, Hatfield was met at the gates of the gaol by one of the Duke's servants, who accompanied him to the harbour, where he was put on the next packet to Holyhead.

Hatfield next came to public attention in 1792 when he arrived in Scarborough, where, as usual, he booked into one of the resort's leading hotels. He again lived off claims of his aristocratic connections, his vast country estates, and the imminent arrival of a large amount of money. His bills of exchange were accepted without hesitation, in the early days at least, but later his lies were revealed. On 25 April he was arrested for failing to pay his hotel bill and found himself in Scarborough's gaol. Some weeks later his whereabouts became known in London, where a warrant was issued in respect of another debt.

There was to be no immediate release on this occasion and he spent the next eight years imprisoned on the Yorkshire coast. That was until 1800, when a Miss Nation, who had travelled north from Devonshire, visited the town. She learnt of Hatfield's imprisonment and visited him regularly. Their relationship flourished, and on 13 September he was released after she had paid his debts. They married the following day and travelled to her home in Tavistock, where, because of his apparent aristocratic connections, and his marriage to the widely respected former Miss Nation, he was welcomed as a partner in the firm of local merchants Messrs Denis & Co.

Unfortunately, despite the comfortable circumstances he now found himself in, Hatfield could not abandon his criminal ways. He swindled the firm out of several hundred pounds, and in April 1802, facing arrest once more, he abandoned his wife and their two children. With his newly acquired capital, he toured Ireland and Scotland, before his arrival in Keswick in the summer.

Upon his arrival in the Lake District he had of course continued in his criminal ways, and was now a fugitive. Having rowed across the lake, he made his way to the coast, and for a few days disguised himself as a sailor, and hid in a small sloop near the shore at Ravenglass. However, he was recognised on 25 October, and took a coach to Ulverston. From there he travelled to Chester, where he was seen in a theatre, necessitating another hasty departure.

A reward notice offering £50 for Hatfield's capture was issued on 8 November, and he was next heard of in Builth, Wales, where he swindled a friend, who was unaware that

Ravenglass, where John Hatfield attempted to hide from his pursuers. (Cumbria County Council)

Hatfield was a wanted man. He headed south, and on 27 November was seen in the hills near Swansea. A search of the area was made, and he was captured the following day in the Lamb and Flag, a coaching inn.

He was taken to Brecon Gaol, where he was detained for two weeks before being escorted to London, to appear before Sir Richard Ford at Bow Street Magistrates Court. He made several appearances and was held in Tothill Fields Prison, where he complained bitterly, as, much to his annoyance, he was forced to associate with those he regarded as being common criminals such as pickpockets and prostitutes. His request for a transfer to Newgate was refused, but his solicitor gave him a weekly allowance of one guinea, which enabled him to live more comfortably. A number of well-known individuals attended the London hearings, curious to see this notorious character, including the Duke of Cumberland and the playwright Monk Lewis.

Hatfield spent Christmas behind bars, and surprisingly, despite all she had learnt of her husband's more recent past, his wife left their children at home in Devonshire to be with him on Christmas Day.

Eventually, it was decided on which charges he would stand trial at Carlisle. The first was in respect of passing a forged bill of exchange upon John Crump for £20 under the false name of Alexander Augustus Hope; the second was for forging a bill of exchange for £30 upon John Crump and payable to Colonel Nathaniel Moore; the third was defrauding the Post Office by franking letters falsely in the name of A.A. Hope, a Member of Parliament, to avoid paying postage. If convicted of these offences he faced execution.

Despite the serious nature of these charges, it was the revelation that he had seduced and bigamously married Mary Robinson that turned public opinion against him. His case was not helped when it became known that she had been pregnant but had suffered a miscarriage. When news of the marriage first became known, his supporters claimed that by refusing to marry the heiress, Miss D., and instead opting to marry the daughter of a humble innkeeper, he had demonstrated that he was not simply an amoral villain out to make money. However, support fell away following revelations that he had not married Miss D., as he feared exposure which would inevitable follow the widespread publicity that would follow such a union, and that he had swindled Mary's parents out of £180. Furthermore, it also emerged that he had attempted to persuade Mr and Mrs Robinson to sell the inn and give him the proceeds so he could invest the money, supposedly on their behalf.

Despite his seduction and betrayal of her, Mary refused to appear in court to testify against him for bigamy, but she was persuaded to write the following letter to Sir Richard Ford:

> Sir, the man whom I had the misfortune to marry and who has ruined me and my aged and unhappy parents, always told me that he was the Honourable Colonel Hope, the next brother of the Earl of Hopetoun.

Early in the New Year, Hatfield was moved to more comfortable accommodation in Newgate. It was from here, aware of the public antipathy towards him, that he wrote an open letter to the press, asking his many detractors not to condemn him before hearing all of the evidence at his forthcoming trial. He was eventually taken to Carlisle Gaol on 25 May to await his appearance at the next assizes, which took place on Monday 15 August, before the notoriously harsh Judge Alexander Thompson. Mr Scarlet prosecuted, and the defendant was represented by Messrs Topping and Holroyd.

Mr Scarlet called several witnesses, the first of which was Mr W. Quick, an employee of Denis & Co. in Tavistock, who identified the accused's handwriting in his letters and on the forged bills of exchange. However, it was the evidence provided by those who had put their trust in Hatfield, and whose sense of betrayal was tangible as they spoke, that was to prove crucially important.

Revd Nicholson told of the several letters he had received from the prisoner, franked with the name A.A. Hope, Member of Parliament, thus avoiding postage, and George Wood and John Crump spoke of the forged bills of exchange. Also called was Colonel Parke, who confirmed the prisoner was not A.A. Hope, who was a close personal friend, and who was abroad.

In his defence, Hatfield called Mr Newton, a lawyer who had represented the prisoner in the past in relation to an estate in Cheshire which he had once owned, and which had made £100 in annual rent. This was an attempt by Hatfield to persuade the jury that he was a man of means who had no need to live by fraud.

However, this defence failed, and following a particularly damning summing up of the evidence by the judge, the jury took just ten minutes to convict him of all the charges. It was now seven o'clock and the trial had begun eight hours earlier, which led the judge to postpone sentence until eight o'clock the following morning, when a packed courtroom heard him address Hatfield thus:

> John Hatfield, after a long and serious investigation of the charges against you, you have been found guilty by a jury of your country. You have been distinguished for crimes of such

Eng.^d by Mackenzie from a Drawing by W Bennet.

Mary of Buttermere.

Mary was able to put the traumatic events of the early years of the nineteenth century behind her and find great happiness. (Author's collection)

magnitude as have seldom, if ever received any mitigation of capital punishment, and in your case it is impossible it can be remitted.

Assuming the person, name and character of a worthy and respectable officer of a noble family in this country, you have perpetrated and committed the most enormous crimes. The long imprisonment you have undergone has afforded you time for your serious reflection and an opportunity of your being deeply impressed with a sense of the enormity of your guilt, and the justice of that sentence which must be inflicted upon you.

I wish you to be seriously impressed with the awfulness of your situation, and to reflect with anxious care and deep concern on your approaching end, concerning which much remains to be done. Lay aside now your delusion and imposition and employ properly the short space of time you have to live. I beseech you to employ the remaining part of your time for eternity, that you may find mercy at the hour of death and in the day of judgement.

He was sentenced to death, but despite the harsh comments of the judge, there was a widespread belief that he would be reprieved. Hatfield, however, seemed resigned to his fate, and spent his time reading the Bible and writing letters to his family and those few friends who had remained loyal. His father and sister did not visit him, and his wife could not afford the cost of travelling from Devonshire. He was in low spirits until his father sent him some money, after which his mood improved greatly, for he could now afford to pay for the luxuries which helped to improve a stay in gaol.

A few days before his execution, he sent for Joseph Bushby, a Carlisle undertaker, to measure him for his coffin. Hatfield dreaded the thought of his corpse being taken by body snatchers, and ordered a plain but very strong oak coffin, saying, 'I request Sir, that after I am taken down, I may be put into the coffin immediately, with the apparel I may have on,

The inn at Buttermere later became known as the Fish Hotel. (Author's collection)

and afterwards closely screwed down, put into the hearse, which will be waiting, carried to the churchyard of Burgh-on-Sands, and there be interred by evening.'

Carlisle executions took place in the afternoon; a tradition which supposedly started after a man was hanged early one morning, only for a reprieve to arrive by the afternoon post. Hatfield's hanging was scheduled for four o'clock on Saturday 3 September 1803, a market day.

That morning, the condemned man rose at six o'clock and spent thirty minutes in the chapel. He returned to his cell and sent for the *Carlisle Journal*, which he read until visited by the Revds Pattison and Mark, with whom he prayed and drank coffee. At ten o'clock his fetters were removed, and clearly not worried that he would attempt suicide, the gaoler allowed him a razor with which to shave.

The afternoon post arrived, but there was no reprieve. Hatfield did not seem unduly concerned, and at three o'clock he ate a splendid meal and drank several glasses of wine with his gaoler. Half an hour later he was pinioned, his bonds being tied loosely at his request, so that once the noose had been placed around his neck, he might signal to the hangman more easily when he was ready to die. He asked to meet the executioner, who had travelled from Dumfries for a fee of ten guineas, and after shaking his hand, Hatfield gave him the last of his money, 2s 6d. Later in the afternoon, the sheriff, bailiffs and Carlisle Yeomanry formed a procession for the fifteen-minute journey to the execution site, at the Sands, to which Hatfield travelled in a post-chaise, accompanied by the gaoler and the executioner.

The scaffold consisted of two posts, 6ft apart, joined by a cross beam, from which the noose dangled. Beneath this was a dung cart, against which a ladder was leaning, and which Hatfield had to climb before the noose could be placed around his neck. The condemned man had decided not to make a speech to the many thousands of spectators who had gathered to watch him die. The crowd watched with some admiration as he calmly assisted the executioner adjust the noose around his neck, before the cart was pulled from under his feet, which was followed by his almost instantaneous death.

His wish that he be buried at Burgh-on-Sands was not carried out, as the villagers refused to allow it. Instead he was buried in the graveyard of St Mary's Church, where Carlisle's executed criminals were usually buried.

As for Mary, she later married a wealthy farmer and became mother to several children. She led an extremely happy life until her death in 1834.

TWO

TWO DESPICABLE CRIMES

⊰ CARLISLE AND GOSFORTH, 1826 ⊱

The Lake District was the setting for two particularly shocking murders in the late summer of 1826, and both victims were young women, who died at the hands of vicious and ruthless men, who were destined to hang together at Carlisle.

Ribbon seller Philip Tinnenay was a young Irishman who made his living by hawking his wares throughout the Lakes, calling door-to-door and visiting fairs and markets. Despite his lack of formal education, he was a talented musician and artist, but was known to have a violent temper.

Tinnenay visited Carlisle regularly, and it was here that he met twenty-six-year-old Mary Brown, described by those who knew her as a young woman of loose morals. When money was short she resorted to prostitution to survive, and she lodged in a house owned by Mary Graham on Botchergate, to which the young ribbon seller became a regular visitor. Mary was not as committed to their relationship as he was, and continued to meet with other men. This angered Tinnenay, who demanded that she stop doing so, but this was how Mary survived, and she made it clear that she had no intention of changing her ways.

Ruth Williamson lived in the room below Mary's, and on Sunday 27 August 1826 an extremely violent argument, was raging above her head. She heard the door to Mary's room open, followed by the sound of her running down the stairs. Ruth opened her door to witness Tinnenay catch hold of Mary, and beat her savagely as she struggled to escape his grip. Mary managed to free herself and flee, and a terrified Ruth slammed her door. Later, when she saw Mary, she urged her to stop seeing Tinnenay, to which her friend replied that she had tried to end the relationship but he would not leave her alone.

The arguments continued, and at midnight on Monday 4 September, Mary Graham heard Tinnenay enter the house. There was no reply when he knocked on Mary's door, as she was hiding from him. She heard him force the door open and enter her room to look for her, but he clearly failed to find her, for seconds later a furious Tinnenay burst into

Top of Botchergate, Carlisle

Botchergate, where Mary Brown had lodgings. (Author's collection)

Mary Graham's room and accused her of harbouring Mary Brown. He threw back the sheets of the bed, believing her to be hiding beneath them. Frustrated when he realised she was not there, he left the house, after which a terrified Mary Brown emerged from the hiding place in her room. She told her landlady that she was now in fear of her life. Tinnenay returned the following morning to confront Mary Brown, and was heard to accuse her once more of seeing other men, and he also threatened to kill her.

On the following Wednesday at ten o'clock, Mary Brown left her lodgings to meet Tinnenay. They were seen walking towards the well on Collier Lane, and later entering Near Hill Field, which led into Far Field. When Mary did not return to her lodgings that night, her landlady presumed that she had been foolish enough to spend the night elsewhere with Tinnenay.

Nothing was seen of either of them until the following afternoon, when a distraught Tinnenay arrived at the room of Ruth Williamson and asked her, 'Where's Mary Brown? Have you seen her? Has she returned? Have you heard anything?' When Ruth replied that she had not seen her since the previous day, Tinnenay broke down and cried, 'I've killed her. I've beaten her. I've hammered her brains out.' On hearing these dreadful words Ruth fainted, and when she had recovered her senses a few minutes later, she found Tinnenay lying on her bed crying. She ran into the street, where she met William Storey, who gathered a number of men together. They approached Tinnenay, demanding to know if he was speaking the truth, and if so, where would they find Mary. He told them to look in Far Field, where he claimed to have left her after beating her unconscious, but added that she was alive when he had left the scene on the previous day.

The men left to search for her, and Tinnenay visited the Jovial Butcher, a public house in Botchergate, where he told the landlady, Ann Irving, that he thought he must have murdered his girlfriend, but could not be certain. He took out his handkerchief and started to cry again, saying, 'They call her Mary Brown; she is a bad woman.' He explained that he had returned from Scotland in the hope of finding her alive.

Meanwhile, William Storey and his group, John Wright, John Burgess and William Thursby, discovered a badly injured Mary in Far Field. She had sustained horrific injuries but was still alive, almost twenty-four hours after suffering the vicious attack. They carried her to her lodgings, where she lingered until her death at three o'clock the following morning.

Earlier, Tinnenay had left the Jovial Butcher and walked to Mary's lodgings, where he was immediately arrested by Constable Felix Rock, who had been told of his confession by Ruth Williamson. He was taken to the Clerk of the Peace's Office where he signed a confession, in which he admitted killing her, and this was witnessed by magistrate Thomas Blantire. It emerged that between two and six o'clock on Wednesday he had plied Mary with rum after she had refused to live with him. He described flying into a rage and hitting her many times about the head with a hammer he had taken with him. He had left the field after first covering her battered face with her apron, and decided to flee to Scotland. He had spent the night in a barn, but decided to return, spurred on by a guilty conscience, and in the hope of finding that she had survived.

The inquest into Mary's death took place before coroner Richard Lowry at the Jovial Butcher on Friday 8 September. The evidence of those who had witnessed the events of the previous few days was heard, together with the testimonies of two local doctors, James Marrs and Railton Atkinson.

They had been called to treat Mary's injuries, and began by shaving her head. They found a piece of her brain protruding from a wound, and Dr Marrs next inserted his finger into three deep head wounds, and discovered three skull fractures. One of her fingers was broken, which had been caused as she had desperately attempted to defend herself.

However, she was beyond help, and following her death the doctors performed a post-mortem. They concluded that any of the three major head wounds could have caused her death, and that the most likely weapon would have been a hammer, although the one Tinnenay claimed to have used was never found as he had thrown it away somewhere along the road to Scotland

Tinnenay listened to the evidence with his head bowed, but became especially distressed when a police officer produced items of Mary's clothing, which she had been wearing at the time of her death, and which included her bloodstained bonnet.

The coroner's jury took five minutes to find the prisoner guilty of wilful murder, and he was taken to Carlisle Gaol to await his trial at the next assizes. This took place on 9 March 1827, after the judge had entered a formal plea of not guilty on his behalf, due to the accused refusing to enter one. The evidence was of course overwhelming, and the jury deliberated for a brief time only before returning with a verdict of guilty. Tinnenay appeared unmoved as he was sentenced to death, but before being led from the dock he asked that a sheet of paper be handed to the judge, on which he had written:

Judgement without mercy, I own is my due,
I murdered the woman, my confession is true.
With me you may do as you please,
In your great hands you hold the keys.
Of life or death,
'Tis one request of you I crave,
Leave not this corruption in a grave.
It would be too great honour on it conferred,
Where Christian bodies are interred.
But hang it up on gibbets high,
Erect between the Earth and Sky.
And let the gibbet rest upon
The ground whereon the wrong was done.
And in that pasture let it stay
Till its glutted on by birds of prey.
To be a warning to further ages,
In hopes to stop such base outrages,
That all who pass that way may see
What human passion brought to me.
That they may tell it with surprise,
'Tis Life for Life did sacrifice.

As Tinnenay's case closed, another murder trial began: that of Robert Fox, who was accused of poisoning his wife.

On Thursday 15 September 1826, Fox entered the shop of Whitehaven druggist David Saul and asked for two pennyworth of arsenic, claiming he wished to kill some rats. Initially, Mr Saul, who at the time was the only member of staff in the shop, refused to serve him. He explained that he did not know Fox and anyway, it was the policy of the shop to have two staff members present when poisons were sold.

However, also in the shop was John James, an old school friend of Fox, who was known to Mr Saul. He vouched for Fox's good character, and Mr Saul therefore agreed to sell him the arsenic. The druggist explained that he never put arsenic on the scales, and he measured out about one and a half ounces of the poison. He wrapped it into three small separate parcels, on all of which he wrote the word 'POISON'. He warned Fox to keep it well away from food and cooking utensils. Fox thanked him and as he left the shop, John James quipped, 'I hope you are not going to poison your wife!'

Fox and his wife Sarah, who was due to give birth to their first child at any moment, lived with her parents John and Mary Pharaoh at Gosforth. On Saturday 17 September, at 5 p.m., John and Mary left the house to attend a christening at a neighbour's house. They had been reluctant to leave their daughter, but Sarah assured them she was feeling well, and Robert would look after her while they were out.

At seven thirty, Fox sought out his mother-in-law, telling her that Sarah was very ill and she should come home immediately. As they walked home Mary attempted to reassure her son-in-law, suggesting that he should not worry as Sarah was probably simply going into labour.

Whitehaven, where Robert Fox purchased the poison he used to murder his wife. (Cumbria County Council)

Ominously, he replied that he thought it was more serious and that he did not think she would survive the night. He added that Mary's youngest daughter, Margaret, was showing similar symptoms, but Mary replied that the youngster was probably only suffering from a cold.

Mary arrived home to be told by Sarah, 'I am very bad, and Bob warmed me some coffee, which was left from morning, and he has put something in it.' He denied this, claiming that, 'She's taking fancies.' However, Margaret had also poured herself a cup of the coffee, and she too had become ill, although she was not suffering as much pain as her older sister. Mary gave the family pig some of the coffee, and almost immediately, it too showed signs of being unwell.

Mary then brewed some hyssop tea for Sarah, who again complained of the bitter taste. Mary decided that the water in the kettle must be to blame, so rinsed it out and made a fresh brew, which Sarah said was delicious. She also told her mother that she was hungry, so Mary made a possett of milk, bread and beer, which Sarah thoroughly enjoyed. She seemed to be improving and Fox suggested that his in-laws should retire to bed, and he would look after Sarah.

Her unsuspecting parents did so, as it was now 2 a.m., but Mary slept only fitfully and five hours later went downstairs to be with her daughter. Sarah told her that after she and her father had gone to bed, her husband had given her the remainder of the possett, but it had tasted more bitter than the serving Mary had given her. Sarah was convinced that her husband had put something in it.

Sarah continued to complain of terrible stomach pains throughout the rest of the day and vomited on several occasions. Early on Sunday morning, Fox called on Dr William

Wright, who, on hearing a description of Sarah's symptoms, gave him some medication for her. However, there was no improvement in her condition and a few hours later the doctor visited her at home. On his arrival he asked to see some of her vomit, as this would help him make a diagnosis, but it had been cleaned up by her husband.

On Sunday evening, Mary realised that Sarah was about to give birth. She called on her friend and neighbour, Mary Briggs and her daughter, also Mary, to help. Sarah went into labour at 4 a.m. and the baby was delivered three hours later. Sadly, the baby, who was exceptionally dark in colour, was stillborn, and Sarah was inconsolable.

Despite drinking large quantities of water and beer, Sarah continued to suffer from a burning throat and chronic stomach pains. Her husband had told a relative that he had bought some special medicine for Sarah on Thursday, to help ease the discomfort of her pregnancy. Sarah had been made aware of this and she therefore knew of the Whitehaven visit. It was now that she must have realised what was happening to her, and in the hearing of her mother, Mary Briggs and her daughter, Sarah accused him of deliberately poisoning her, which Fox vehemently denied. Nevertheless she persisted, saying to him:

> You did, and you bought the stuff in Whitehaven on Thursday. You have poisoned me and killed my child, but killing me is nothing to killing my child. I freely forgive you Bob, and I hope God Almighty will forgive me my sins, and I expect that you will suffer as much on earth as I have.

She continued to suffer for a further two days before eventually dying on Tuesday evening.

Gosforth. (Cumbria County Council)

Carlisle Gaol. (Cumbria County Council)

The inquest into Sarah's death was held on 23 and 24 September before coroner William Bragg. The jury heard evidence from those who had witnessed the events in the hours before her death, together with details of the post-mortem performed by Whitehaven surgeons Mr Lawson and Mr Thomson, who had carefully examined her mouth, tongue, throat and the contents of her stomach. They had no hesitation in concluding that she had been poisoned, and nor did the jury in declaring that Fox was guilty of her murder, after which he was taken from Gosforth to Carlisle Gaol to await his trial.

At the assizes, he entered the dock after Tinnenay, but did not face trial for the attempted murder of his wife's sister, Margaret, as it was accepted by the prosecution that she had not been an intended victim, and he had not given her the poisoned coffee. The outcome was of course never really in doubt, and having listened to the evidence, and without leaving their seats, the jury found him guilty of Sarah's murder.

Having listened to the judge sentence him to death, the phlegmatic Fox addressed the jury, saying:

> Well gentlemen, I am quite satisfied with the decision to which you have come. I am quite willing to give up mine for the life I have taken. The taking of the wife's life is nothing to taking the life of the child. I hope for no favour, for no mercy. The Lord brought me into the world and I hope he will take me out of it.

Fox was taken to the condemned cell at Carlisle Gaol, to await his execution two days later, no motive having been established or offered for the crime.

The two condemned men had been held in custody for several months and Tinnenay had spent much of his time with the gaol's priest. Fox had entered the gaol illiterate, but took literacy classes and was able to read and write by the time of his trial. A meeting had been arranged with John and Mary Pharaoh, and these good, decent people were able to forgive him for the murder of their daughter.

There was little public sympathy for either of the two men. It was acknowledged that Tinnenay had been responsible for a crime of passion, and that he had returned in the hope of possibly saving his victim's life, but there were indications that there had been an element of planning. He had rum ready to give her after she had refused to live with him, with the intention of getting her drunk, which would have made attacking her that much easier. He also had the weapon with him, which seemingly he had taken to use against her. Sarah Fox had been condemned to a prolonged and painful death, which had been compounded by the physical and emotional stress of delivering a stillborn child as she lay dying, and realising that her husband was responsible.

At noon on Monday 11 March 1827, the two murderers, their arms already pinioned, were taken from the condemned cell, through a room lined with sheriffs' officers, to the place of execution. A crowd of many thousands had gathered to watch the hangings, and the first to be placed on the drop was Fox. He was dressed rather drably in a corduroy waistcoat and trousers, as he had given his best clothes, in which he had been tried, to a friend. He was followed by Tinnenay, who wore an old blue coat.

The noose was placed around Fox's neck, and a white cap was pulled down over his head. He was required to stand like this for several minutes as Tinnenay prayed with the priest. Eventually, he too was ready for the execution, and after they fell through the drop, the two bodies were left swinging in a strong wind for an hour before being cut down.

Tinnenay's wish to be gibbeted was not complied with. Instead, his corpse, along with that of Fox, was taken back into the gaol, and their bodies were dissected in front of a gathering of eminent medical men and their students.

THREE

THE MICHAELMAS FAIR MURDER

⚵ COCKERMOUTH, 1833 ⚵

Nineteenth-century fairs were hugely important, both economically and socially, in the life of a village or town, and were often raucous occasions. The Michaelmas Fair at Cockermouth was no exception, and in 1833 it provided the backdrop to a brutal murder.

On the morning of Thursday 10 October, Bernard Burns, a twenty-four-year-old collier who lived in Workington, left the home of his parents, with whom he lived, and travelled to Cockermouth, intent on enjoying the delights of the fair. However, he did not return home that night, and was missing for several days. That was until the following Thursday, when his body was discovered in the River Derwent.

The body was carried to his parents' house, where a post-mortem was performed. He was found to have suffered a number of serious injuries, which included a large cut to his left temple and small cuts to the right side of his head, and to his left eyebrow. He had obviously been dead for about seven days, and it was believed that the injuries were consistent with his having suffered a severe beating. At the inquest, which was held on 19 October, foul play was suspected, but no witnesses had come forward who could provide information as to how he met his death, and there was no evidence linking the death to anyone else. This was seemingly a mystery to which no satisfactory explanation would be found.

However, several months later, Margaret Thompson came forward and named five local men whom she claimed were responsible for murdering Bernard Burns. The circumstances surrounding Bernard's death are best told by describing the five criminal trials that followed in 1834 and 1835.

The men named by Margaret were twenty-nine-year-old Thomas Nicholson, his cousins William and Walter Nicholson, aged twenty-two and nineteen respectively, Joseph Green, aged twenty-eight, and twenty-two-year-old John Burgess. They were all colliers who had known the dead man, but there was no history of bad blood between them and the deceased, and no immediately obvious motive for his murder.

Cockermouth. (Author's collection)

Workington, the home town of Bernard Burns. (Cumbria County Council)

Lord Lyndhurst, the trial judge.
(Author's collection)

They were arraigned before the trial judge, Lord Lyndhurst, at the Cumberland Assizes of August 1834. The prosecution barristers were Sergeant Atcherley and Mr Armstrong, while Sir Gordon Gregory defended the three Nicholsons, and Mr Knowles represented Green and Burgess.

The first and by far the most important prosecution witness was Margaret Thompson, a prostitute who had visited the fair to ply her trade. She began by telling the court that she knew the deceased, and had seen him in Cowen's beer tent in the early evening, and again at midnight in Hodgson's tent. At this later meeting he told her that he had been in a scrape earlier in the day and had been struck on the head by one of the local constables, who had told him to behave himself. He had given no further details but she felt a large bump on his head, and he said he was feeling dizzy. They parted when a gentleman she had arranged to meet arrived, but she saw Bernard again two hours later. He waved at her, shouting that he was going home, and she then heard him say 'Hello' to the five accused, who were approaching him.

She continued her testimony by saying that without any apparent warning, Bernard was seized around the neck by Green, who cursed him before hitting him. This caused him to fall to the ground, and as Bernard attempted to rise to his feet, he held out his hand to his attacker, saying, 'Joe my lad, I'll not fight. I am so stupid with the blow I received earlier. I'll shake hands and be friends.' He offered to buy a drink for Green, who responded by knocking him to the ground again. Once more, Bernard tried to stand, but as he did so, he was struck across the back of the head with a whip by Thomas Nicholson.

Concerned for Bernard's safety, Margaret ran towards the group of men, begging them to stop the assault. Green swore at her and shouted, 'If you don't go away I'll smash your brains out as small as an egg was ever chopped for a canary!' Now fearing for her own welfare, Margaret ran away, but watched from a distance as the beating continued.

She heard Green demand that Bernard fight him, but again the injured man refused, but promised to do so in the future as he attempted to walk away. However, he was followed by the five men, and at this point Margaret was joined by another gentleman who had arranged to see her, and they both watched as the five men forced Bernard into a field.

They saw Green strike his victim again, and it was clear that Bernard was becoming increasingly weaker and more confused. Thomas Nicholson once more used his whip on him and Bernard could be heard begging for mercy. After falling to the ground, one of the men exclaimed, 'By God, he is done!' Thomas Nicholson and Joseph Green picked him up and carried him towards the riverbank. Their three companions followed and a few moments later Margaret and her friend heard a loud splash. The man grabbed her hand and pulled her away, saying, 'For God's sake, come on, or we will be next.'

Later, Margaret met Edward Parkin, and agreed to spend a few hours with him at the house of Margaret Simm, who allowed them to sleep in one of her bedrooms. Shortly after their arrival, Margaret Thompson heard a church clock strike five o'clock.

The bridge spanning the River Derwent. (Cumbria County Council)

Margaret Thompson was cross-examined at length by the defence barristers and admitted that she was a prostitute, and had served two prison sentences for theft. She acknowledged that she had not contacted the constables at the time of Bernard's disappearance, and furthermore, she had not attended the inquest, despite knowing it was being held. When asked for an explanation, she replied that she had been warned not to speak out against the five defendants, but later she had decided that she should report what she had seen to the authorities.

The second witness to be called was Richard Black, a local tailor, who on the day of the fair had been working as a waiter at the Sun Inn. He told the jury that shortly after midnight he was standing at the entrance to the inn when he saw the five accused and Bernard. He watched as they forced him into the field, and he could see Thomas Nicholson and Joseph Green strike their victim, forcing him to the ground. As they did so he heard one of the accused men scream, 'By God, thou shall either fight or else we'll take thy life!'

When questioned by the defence lawyers, he acknowledged that he had not informed the constables of what he had seen, and could offer no explanation other than not wanting to become involved. Nevertheless, he had decided to come forward after learning that Margaret Thompson had done so. The defence lawyers poured scorn on this explanation, and claimed that he was lying, just as Margaret Thompson had lied. They cast further doubt on his reliability when he admitted that he did not know what month of the year they were now in.

At Michaelmas Fair time, all of Cockermouth's main thoroughfares, including Station Street, were lined with stalls selling all types of wares and alcohol. (Cumbria County Council)

The prosecution called a number of other witnesses who had not come forward at the time of Bernard's death, but their evidence supported the Crown's claim that the five men were in each other's company in the early hours of the morning. Edward Campbell stated that he had seen the group at 2 a.m.; John Bowman and Jonathon Corry testified that they had seen them between midnight and 1 a.m.; William Wordsworth, a relative of the great poet, told the court that he had also seen Burgess in the company of Joseph Allison Junior at midnight.

Also called to testify was fourteen-year-old Esther Taylor, who described walking past the field in question at 4 a.m. on her way to work at a local mill. She noticed a trail of blood in the field leading to the river bank, in which the assault was said to have occurred, giving credence to the Crown's case that a vicious assault had recently taken place there. When asked by the defence why she had not reported this earlier, she replied that her father had told her not to do so.

The five men had denied any knowledge of the crime from the moment they were arrested, and the statements they had given at the time were read out to the court. Thomas Nicholson claimed not to have seen his co-accused on the day of the fair, and that he had spent the night at the home of his father-in-law, Nathan Todd. Joseph Green acknowledged that he had met the dead man earlier in the day, but insisted he had not seen him that night, and he had slept at the home of Robert and Hannah Ostle. Walter and William Nicholson also claimed not to have seen Bernard on the day of the fair, and stated that they had slept at the home of their father from 10 p.m. until 7 a.m. John Burgess recalled seeing Bernard during the day, but had not seen him later, had not met the four other accused, and had gone to bed at 9 p.m.

The defence began by attempting to discredit the testimony of Margaret Thompson, whose character and honesty they had already called into question when cross-examining her. Those representing the accused now called witnesses to support the claim that she could not possibly have seen the events she had described and had thus lied to the court.

Edward Parkin testified that he had met Margaret at eight o'clock on the night of the fair, and that they were together for the next ten hours, except for the period between eight thirty and nine thirty. After enjoying the delights of the fair, they arrived at the home of Margaret Simm at one o'clock in the morning, and she allowed them to sleep in one of her rooms. Parkin continued his evidence by insisting that Margaret Thompson had not left the bed at any time that night.

Margaret Simm was the next to be called into the witness box, and she testified that the previous witness and Margaret Thompson had shared a bed at her home until he had left the house at 6 a.m. and she had left three hours later. She insisted that neither of her guests could have left the house at any time without her knowing.

Edward Campbell claimed to have seen the five accused together at 2 a.m., but the defence produced Hugh Mackavey, who stated this could not have been so as he had been with Campbell between 11 p.m. and 6 a.m., together with Hugh Brittain and John Cape. They had found a hay loft to sleep in, and throughout the whole of that time the four of them had not been out of each other's sight for more than ten minutes, meaning that Edward Campbell could not possibly have seen the five men at the time he claimed to have done so.

Mr Knowles next called members of the Allison family, who provided alibi evidence on behalf of Burgess. Joseph Allison Snr, who was at the fair with his wife and daughter, told of meeting Burgess at Thompson's public house. The witness had later invited him to stay at his home for the night, and the offer of hospitality had been accepted. When the two men reached the Allison home, they had smoked their pipes before falling asleep in their chairs. They were awakened at midnight, when Joseph Allison Jnr arrived home. The young Allison and his friend, Burgess, slept together in Allison's bed until seven o'clock in the morning. When called to give evidence, young Allison confirmed these details and insisted that Burgess could not have left the bed without his knowledge.

Sarah Allison confirmed the evidence given by her husband and son. Furthermore, she testified that before going to bed, she had locked the door to the house, and as this was a spring lock nobody could have left without her being aware of it. The Allisons' daughter testified that she had passed her brother's bedroom during the night to give her younger sister a glass of water. She saw her brother and the defendant asleep in the bed, and when she passed the room a few hours later, both young men were still asleep in the bed.

Mr Knowles next called witnesses to prove that Joseph Green could not have been involved in an assault on the deceased. John Johnson insisted that early that evening, he, Robert Ostle and Green had several drinks before being joined later by the accused's wife. After a few more drinks, the group returned to Green's home, where his wife prepared supper. Green and his wife retired to their bed, and the witness, together with Robert and Hannah Ostle, slept together in one bed. The witness concluded his evidence by stating it would have been impossible for Green to have left the house without waking him.

The jury heard Hannah Ostle testify that she and her husband had dined with Green and his wife, and afterwards all four visited the fair. She also backed the evidence of John Johnson, as did Robert Ostle, who followed his wife into the witness box.

The defence witnesses had clearly damaged the Crown's case, and the prosecution called Isabella Frazer in an attempt to refute the evidence of Edward Parkin. If the jury believed her, this would by implication discredit the other defence witnesses. Isabella was the sister of Margaret Thompson, and she knew Edward Parkin well. She recalled a conversation she had with him a few weeks before the trial, in which he had told her that he had been with Margaret in the early part of the evening, but they had separated for several hours, before meeting again later and visiting Margaret Simm's house. He had also told her that he did not know where her sister was during the hours they were apart.

In his summing up, the judge drew the jury's attention to the conflicting evidence they had been presented with, and that it was for them to decide which of the witnesses they believed. The jury retired for forty minutes and returned with 'not guilty' verdicts in respect of all of the accused. This was met with a stunned silence in the courtroom, and the judge threw himself back in his chair, as though surprised at the outcome. He addressed the five men by saying, 'Prisoners, since the jury have thought proper to acquit you, you are entitled to be discharged. Let them be discharged.' Thus the trial came to an end after twelve hours.

Outside, a crowd of several thousand had assembled in the surrounding streets to await the verdicts, which were expected to be guilty in all five cases. When the outcome of the trial became known, astonishment turned almost immediately to anger. The gaoler, Mr Orridge, advised the men of the crowd's ugly mood, and urged them to wait a few hours before leaving the courthouse. The men refused to heed this wise advice, and demanded to be released immediately. The gaoler released them and, as it was now dark, they were not recognised immediately.

COCKERMOUTH MURDER.

AN ACCOUNT

OF THE

TRIAL AND ACQUITTAL

OF THOMAS NICHOLSON, WILLIAM NICHOL-
SON, WALTER NICHOLSON, JOSEPH
GREEN, AND JOSEPH BURGESS,

CHARGED WITH

The Murder of Bernard Burns,

At COCKERMOUTH, on the 10th October, 1833,

TRIED AT CARLISLE,

ON TUESDAY, AUGUST 6TH, 1834,

Before Lord LYNDHURST;

WITH THE

JUDGE'S CHARGE, AND NAMES OF THE JURY.

(Taken from the Carlisle Patriot, August 9th, 1834.)

CARLISLE:
PRINTED FOR JAMES PALL, BY HUDSON SCOTT.

Price Two Pence.

Transcripts of murder trials were popular at the time and sold in large numbers. (Author's collection)

They entered Mrs Purdy's public house, which was situated directly opposite the main entrance to the courthouse, and were recognised on entering the premises. Green was heard to swear revenge against the prosecution witnesses, and Thomas Nicholson struck his wife a violent blow across her face as she approached him, cursing her for failing to give evidence on his behalf.

Once the crowd realised where the released men were, a large number rushed Mrs Purdy's house and dragged the five of them out into the street, where they were savagely beaten. The five managed to free themselves and ran along English Street, and after a short distance they separated.

Walter and William Nicholson managed to flee the town and therefore avoided any further beatings. Their companions, however, were not so fortunate. Green was overtaken by a group of men who beat him mercilessly before he and his wife managed to run into the Turk's Head on Fisher Street, bolting the door as they entered. The landlord was able to summon a constable, who arrived a few minutes later to find Green trembling violently and showing marks from the beating he had just suffered. It was feared that the enraged crowd would burn down the inn, and the constable decided to take the couple to the police office for their own safety. As they left the inn, a number of men nearly prevented their quarry from reaching safety, but Green and his wife were eventually able to get to the sanctuary of the police office.

Burgess, meanwhile, reached the Black Swan, having been badly beaten en route. The landlord insisted he leave, fearing that the angry crowd outside would tear down the inn. Fortunately, Burgess escaped Carlisle, unseen in the dark of night, without suffering any more injuries.

Thomas Nicholson and his wife were recognised by another group of enraged residents as they ran down Paternoster Row. A stone was thrown at him but it struck his wife on her head, and, stunned, she fell to the ground. She soon recovered and she and her husband began running once more, but they were soon cornered. Thomas was subjected to another severe beating, and begged for mercy, but his attackers mocked him and screamed that he had shown none to Bernard Burns. Several constables had been alerted and arrived just in time to save his life. He and his wife were escorted to a house, where they remained for the night, and the constables were able to disperse the crowd by telling them that Nicholson had left by a side door. The following morning he was reunited with his cousins, Green and Burgess, and together with their families they headed for Cockermouth.

Despite their experiences of the previous night, when they almost lost their lives, the five men and their companions entered Cockermouth arm-in-arm, laughing at those who booed and shouted insults at them. Thomas Nicholson struck a boy who was booing him, and later that day he was heard to boast that it was he who had delivered the fatal blow to Bernard Burns. However, there was to be no repeat of the events at Carlisle.

Nevertheless, the reaction of the crowd at Carlisle was a manifestation of the widespread feeling that the five men had literally got away with murder. This was not however confined to the general public alone, for almost immediately the not guilty verdicts had been announced the defence witnesses became the focus of an investigation by the authorities, who also believed five murderers had avoided justice. It was as a result of these enquires that Hannah Ostle, Joseph Allison Senior and Junior, together with Margaret Simm, appeared at the August Assizes of 1835, before Chief Justice Tindal, charged with perjury. Each was tried separately.

The first to be placed in the dock was Hannah Ostle, and the Crown began by reminding the jury of her evidence at the murder trial, which had suggested that she had been in the company of Green and his wife at the fair, which implied that he could not have been present when Bernard Burns allegedly suffered his fatal wounds. However, it was the Crown's intention to persuade the jury that she had lied, and that Green had been one of those responsible for the crime.

Margaret Thompson was called to repeat the evidence she had given at the original trial, stating that Green had participated in the murder. Several other witnesses were called, who testified that they had seen Green that night, and these included William Lowther and his sister Elizabeth, who told the court that Green, together with Robert Ostle and John Johnson, had visited their father's house at half past midnight on the night in question.

No witnesses were called by those representing Ostle, and instead an attempt was made to discredit Margaret Thompson, based on her being a prostitute and former convict. The evidence of the new witnesses was called into question as they had failed to appear at the inquest into Bernard's death, nor had they testified at the murder trial. The absence of Black, whose testimony at the murder trial had supported that of Margaret Thompson, was said to be suspicious, nor had the man who was allegedly with her at the time of the beating been called at any time in the history of the case. The defence also pointed out that the accused's husband, Robert, had given evidence at the trial of the five men, which corroborated that of their client. However, the rules of evidence meant that being her husband he could not be called at her trial to repeat that supporting testimony.

The defence lawyer concluded his evidence by suggesting that all of the prosecution witnesses were unreliable, as, 'We all know that persons of the class of life in which these witnesses are, take no count of time, and are often out in their calculations.'

The jury retired for thirty minutes and found her guilty. The judge postponed sentencing her until the other perjury trials had been completed. As Hannah Ostle was led from the dock she screamed, 'I isn't guilty of perjury. It is all true that I said. I is innocent!'

The second defendant to stand trial was Joseph Allison Snr, who had provided alibi evidence on behalf of Burgess. The Crown again called Margaret Thompson and a number of other witnesses who testified that they had seen Burgess elsewhere on the night in question. William Lowther, for instance, claimed to have seen Burgess at 11.15 p.m. at Hannah Hodgson's public house. The defence once again called no witnesses of their own, and made an attempt to discredit those who had been called by the prosecution. However, the jury took only a few minutes to find the defendant guilty of perjury.

Joseph Allison Jnr fared no better than his father, after a number of witnesses had again testified that they had seen Burgess and this defendant on the streets of Cockermouth in the early hours of the morning, so they could not have been in bed as he had claimed at the murder trial. Once more, there was no strong defence put to the jury, who convicted the defendant of perjury without leaving their seats.

The last defendant to stand trial was Margaret Simm, whose testimony at the murder trial had been used by the defence to discredit that provided by Margaret Thompson. Again the prosecution called a number of witnesses to prove that the defendant had lied at the trial, including Hannah Messenger and Edward Campbell, who both swore that they had seen Margaret Thompson between the hours of midnight and three in the morning, in Cockermouth.

The defence tried a new strategy by claiming that the accused was simply mistaken, and her original evidence, which although possibly wrong, was given in good faith. The jury took thirty minutes to convict her, but there was a recommendation for leniency in her case because of her youth.

The perjury trials having ended, the judge called for the four prisoners to be placed together in the dock. He reminded them of the seriousness of the crime of perjury, especially in murder cases, and expressed some surprise that the jury had asked him to be lenient in the case of Margaret Simm. Nevertheless, he agreed to comply with the request and sentenced her to two years imprisonment with hard labour. The other three defendants were ordered to serve six months in gaol with hard labour, after which they were to be transported to Australia for seven years. All continued to protest their innocence as they were led to the cells. Officially, the murder of Bernard Burns remained unsolved, but there is little doubt who had been responsible in the eyes of the public and the authorities.

It is not known what happened to all of those involved in this case, but on 19 January 1841 the *Cumberland Pacquet* reported that Hannah Ostle had been pardoned eight days earlier, having spent the previous five and a half years in Carlisle Gaol.

FOUR

THE BEWCASTLE MURDER

⚔ BEWCASTLE, 1849 ⚔

Bewcastle lies to the east of the Lakes, which in the first half of the nineteenth century could only be reached by poorly maintained roads, making it an isolated village set amid marshland and heaths. Strangers were met with suspicion and hostility and it was an area inhabited by many criminals, especially poachers.

One of those whose task it was to counter the threat of the gangs of poachers was fifty-two-year-old Thomas Davidson, who had been employed as a game watcher by Sir James Graham of Netherby Hall since the early 1830s. Thomas and his family lived at Kettle Hall, which despite its grandiose name, was a small cottage on the Netherby estate.

He worked under gamekeeper John Armstrong, who, on Thursday 8 November 1849, had arranged to collect Thomas and accompany him for the day. However, John had not arrived by 9 a.m., and Thomas decided to set off without him. A few minutes later the gamekeeper arrived and left a message with Tom's wife, Margaret, to say he would call the next morning. However, Thomas did not return home that night, nor had he done so by the time John called on Friday morning. Family and friends organised a search, but could find no trace of him that day.

It was the following day, 10 November, that the game watcher's body was found on the Fells, two miles from his home. His body was lying face down on the ground, and when he was turned over on to his back, it was immediately obvious that he had been the victim of a savage beating.

Having been informed of the crime, the Carlisle police sent Superintendent John Sabbage and two constables to Bewcastle to conduct the investigation. Margaret advised the Superintendent that, when he left home on Thursday morning, her husband had been carrying a relatively large amount of cash, as a few days earlier he had received £7 wages which he had been owed, and he had put most of this in his purse. The money was missing, but Superintendent Sabbage felt that robbery had probably not been the prime motive for the murder. He believed Thomas had probably been attacked by a gang of poachers he had confronted, who had taken the money having found it on his body after they had killed him.

Bewcastle. (Cumbria County Council)

The police quickly focused their attention on a notorious local poacher, Joseph Hogg, who had been heard to threaten the deceased. On Saturday 26 October, Hogg had been convicted of shooting game without a certificate, and had been fined £3 8s, due largely to the testimony of Thomas Davidson. As he was paying the fine, immediately after the court hearing, Hogg uttered a number of oaths and threats against Thomas. One of those who had heard him was John Steel, a reporter with the *Carlisle Journal*, who made a shorthand note of the following threat uttered by the aggrieved poacher in the local dialect, 'That'll do him varra muckle gude I expect, and I'll do for him.'

Twenty-four-year-old Hogg, his twenty-six-year-old cousin, John Nichol, who was also known as Hogg, and Andrew Turnbull, who was in his mid-thirties, had been seen in the vicinity of the murder and were detained. The alibis they attempted to provide for each other were contradictory and they were charged with the game watcher's murder.

The inquest was held in a small upstairs room of the Lyne House Inn at Bewcastle, before the coroner Mr W. Carrick. As the hearing proceeded, the downstairs bar remained open, and there was an almost carnival-like atmosphere as the drunken locals, who had little sympathy for the dead game watcher and his kind, celebrated his death, and toasted the health of whoever had been responsible.

Netherby Hall. (Author's collection)

Christianbury Crags. (Cumbria County Council)

Local surgeon Matthew Patterson performed a post-mortem at Kettle Hall on the Saturday following the discovery of the body. He found the face and neck to be heavily bruised and swollen; Thomas had a black eye and the bridge of his nose was disfigured; his entire upper body showed signs of a savage beating, and the injuries were such that the surgeon believed they had probably been inflicted by more than one person. He had been strangled by his own handkerchief, and an injury to his abdomen led Mr Patterson to conclude that one of the assailants had knelt on him as the handkerchief was tightened around his neck.

Of the accused men, only Turnbull made the difficult seventeen-mile journey to the inquest from Carlisle Gaol. He opted to give evidence, and as he entered the witness box, the coroner reminded him that, 'You are not bound to state anything which might 'criminate yourself in this inquiry. With that caution I shall now examine you, telling you that you are quite at liberty to withhold anything which shows you were a guilty party in the death of Davidson.'

Turnbull gave his evidence in a clear and firm voice, and began his account at seven thirty on the morning of the murder, when Hogg called at his home. He told Turnbull that he and Nichol were going to Christianbury Crags in search of game, and Turnbull agreed to go with them, hoping that he would be able to earn 10s. Turnbull claimed to have expressed his concern that Davidson might be in that area looking for poachers, but Hogg told him that he should not worry himself about the game watcher.

They called at Nichol's house and the three men trekked to Christianbury Crags, but game was scarce and so they moved on. It was one o'clock in the afternoon when they decided to rest, and it was then that Hogg told Turnbull that he and Nichol had decided that if they encountered Thomas Davidson either that day or on another future occasion, they would kill him. In his evidence at the inquest, Turnbull claimed he told his companions that he would not help them, but continued by promising that he would do nothing to prevent them from carrying out the deed, nor would he inform on them. By two thirty they had shot three brace of grouse and a number of other birds, and Turnbull was given 4s as his share. They decided to head for home, but the gunshots had been heard by the game watcher, who Turnbull saw about 60 yards away, walking towards them.

The men began to run away but Turnbull stated that after about 100 yards, Nichol stopped and shouted to Hogg, 'Stop, I'll shoot him!' Turnbull insisted that he continued to run further from the spot, and as he did so he claimed to have heard Nichol shout after him, 'Damn thee, thou'll not run away that way.' However, Turnbull insisted that he continued running for another 50 yards and threw his gun to the ground.

Turnbull heard Thomas call out, 'Hey boys, what's brought you here?' and by now he had closed on the two poachers. Hogg shouted, 'Damn thee, I'll give thee a good thrashing', and Turnbull watched as Hogg lunged at the game watcher, taking his stick from his hand, before punching him fiercely in the face. Thomas told his assailant, 'Give over Joe, and it'll be better for you.' Hogg's response was to grab him by the throat, and as Thomas gasped for breath the game watcher said, 'Give over Joe, thou'll not murder me will you?' The assault continued and Hogg screamed, 'Thou's cost us a deal of money and trouble, but damn thee it shall be the last time.'

Hogg called out to Nichol to help him, and after throwing his gun to the ground, he rushed towards the struggling men. Turnbull continued to watch as the cousins strangled their victim with his own handkerchief. When they had completed their task, Hogg called out to Turnbull, 'Why did you stand there, you are only a faint-hearted bugger at the best,' and continued by warning him not to inform on them.

According to Turnbull, it was Nichol who suggested robbing the dead man, and on searching the body they found his purse, which contained three sovereigns and fifteen half crowns, which the three men shared equally before making their way home. Turnbull told the inquest that from his share he settled a bill owing to tailor Robert Davidson, and spent most of what remained on drink at John Routledge's inn at Clattering Ford.

It was hardly surprising that after a brief time consulting each other, the coroner's jury returned a verdict of guilty to wilful murder against the three accused men, and Turnbull was ordered to be returned to Carlisle Gaol to await trial. During the return coach journey, Turnbull rather naively, expressed surprise and disappointment that he had not been released on bail until the assizes. He told his guard that he was not looking forward to being detained in a cell for any length of time. The carriage reached the gaol at just after nine o'clock at night, and Turnbull was returned to his cell.

Late in the evening of Tuesday 4 December, Mr J. T. Orridge, the governor of Carlisle Gaol, received formal notification of the committal of the three accused to stand trial for murder. The gaol was now in darkness and the men locked in their cells, probably asleep, and he decided to wait until morning before advising them of the news that they were already aware of anyway. At nine thirty the next morning, accompanied by the turnkey, Joseph Gallagher, the governor entered Turnbull's cell, to find him sat on his stool reading the Bible. The prisoner, when told of the committal, repeated his claim of innocence, but there was nothing in his demeanour to suggest any cause for concern. At five o'clock that evening, Joseph visited the cell once more to give the prisoner his supper. They spoke briefly, and in response to the turnkey, Turnbull said he was well.

Joseph next unlocked the cell at a few minutes before seven the following morning. He was carrying a small lamp, which only partially illuminated the dark cell. Turnbull was nowhere to be seen, and the bed had obviously not been slept in. Joseph looked into the partitioned water closet, but seeing no sign of the prisoner, his first thought was that he must have escaped. However, when he lit up the rest of the cell, he saw Turnbull at the window, and at first thought he was going to attack him, but very quickly realised that the prisoner was dead, having hanged himself.

Joseph hurried to the governor's room and found Mr Orridge still asleep. He shook him, exclaiming, 'A bad job has happened sir; Turnbull is dead.' On reaching the cell, the governor could see that Turnbull had tied his towel around one of the bars at the window. The stool had apparently been kicked away from under his feet, which were three inches from the floor. His hands were cold and he had been dead for several hours. He was fully clothed except for his top coat, and as he had not slept in his bed, it was surmised he had committed suicide within minutes of the cell door being locked the previous evening. Scuff marks on the cell wall close to the floor indicated that he had died only after a prolonged and painful struggle.

He was cut down, and the governor commented on what he thought was a large amount of tobacco in his mouth, but was in fact his badly discoloured and swollen tongue. It was then that the governor and turnkey noticed that Turnbull had written three messages on the cell walls with a burnt stick.

Below the cell window he had written: 'The two Hoggs are guilty. I am innocent. I will not come in the hands of man.' Above the fireplace another message read: 'I commit my soul to God that gave it. Take my body to my father's burial place.' The third message was written on the wall above his bed and was intended for his wife: 'My dear, you and I was lovely, but I am torn from thy breast. Don't weep for me.'

The inquest into Turnbull's death was held on Friday 7 December at the Three Crowns in Carlisle. The coroner was Mr Carrick, who only a short time previously had heard the deceased's testimony at the inquest into Thomas Davidson's murder. The coroner asked the governor if it was normal practice for a prisoner such as Turnbull, awaiting trial for his life, to have a towel in his cell. Mr Orridge confirmed that this was the case, but if there had been any concerns raised from his demeanour, arrangements would have been made to have another prisoner put in the cell to prevent such an occurrence.

After all the evidence had been heard, Mr Carrick advised the jury that there could be no explanation other than that Turnbull had committed suicide, and all that they had to determine was his state of mind at the time he made the decision to do so. The jury consulted for a few minutes and decided that Turnbull had indeed committed suicide, but there was no evidence to show his state of mind at the time he hanged himself.

Turnbull's distraught widow, Jemima, was unable to comply with his request that he be buried alongside his father. The prison authorities raised no objection, but she was now destitute and could not afford the costs involved. She possessed just one cow, which she was prepared to sell to raise the necessary funds, but was persuaded by friends and family from doing so, and her husband was buried in the graveyard of Christ Church on Botchergate in Carlisle.

The assizes opened on Saturday 23 February 1850, and the trial of Hogg and Nichol was listed to be heard before the trial judge, Baron Alderson, with Mr Murphy prosecuting and Mr James representing the defendants. However, the trials' opening was delayed due to problems with selecting the jury, which the clerk was about to empanel by the newly introduced method of ballot. However, he was prevented from doing so by the judge, who complained:

I won't have the jury elected out of the ordinary course. The law requires that they should be called by the list sent in by the Sherriff, and why should the ballot box be introduced at all? I don't like these new-fangled ways of securing justice. If the Parliament choose to make a different arrangement, let them do so. Until then I shall adhere to the ancient customs of the country.

The jury was therefore selected in the traditional manner, but not without difficulty and further delay. Jury member John Twentyman asked to be excused, explaining that he had previously employed one of the accused and had found him to be an honest and industrious young man, making it difficult to judge him under the current circumstances. Baron Alderson agreed to this request, and Robert Armstrong was the replacement juror. However, when his name was called out there was no response, and the judge fined him £20 in his absence. Mr Twentyman was ordered to return to his seat with the other jury members, who were eventually sworn in.

The murder charge was put to the defendants, who pleaded not guilty, and at this stage of the proceedings Robert Armstrong entered the courtroom. He explained that he had been waiting in an adjoining court, but as the jury had already been sworn, he could not replace Mr Twentyman. He took his leave after his fine had been reduced to £1.

When the trial began the judge made some preliminary observations concerning the evidence the jury would hear. He made it clear that although he would admit a verbatim account of Turnbull's testimony given at the coroner's court, he had serious reservations about it, given that he would not be available for cross-examination. Nevertheless, although largely circumstantial, the Crown believed it had a good case and could prove the accused were guilty of murder.

Turnbull's widow confirmed that the accused men had called for her late husband on the morning in question, and that on his return he had informed her that they had murdered the game watcher. William Little, a farmer of Stoneknowgate, who described himself as a good friend of the accused men, admitted that he had often sold poached game on their behalf. A few days after the alleged murder, they had asked him to sell three brace of grouse – a small pigeon and a black cock, which was similar in all respects to the description Turnbull had given to the police of the birds shot – to Jane Thompson of Carlisle, a dealer in game, for 11s 3d.

When arrested, Hogg was seen to have scratches to his upper lip, as though he had been involved in a struggle, and blood was found on the breeches and coat he had been seen wearing on the day the murder took place. The police also located witnesses who saw the two men on the following Saturday, in a public house, spending large amounts of cash on drink. Furthermore, Hogg was discovered to have bought an expensive watch for cash from another customer in the bar.

Sergeant John Cowen, assisted by Constable Matthew Snowden and Robert Telford of the North Tyne and Reedwater Association for the Prevention of Poaching and Prosecution of Felons, had gathered what the Crown considered to be incriminating evidence at the murder scene. The officers had taken the boots of Turnbull, Hogg and Nichol, together with those of the murdered man, which each had been thought to have been wearing on the day of the murder. When they were compared with footprints found in the vicinity of the crime, all, with the exception of Hogg's, were found to correspond exactly. The footprints were found over a widespread area, and pointed to a chase of more than a mile from where the poachers were first seen by the game watcher, to the spot where the murder was committed.

Thus, the prosecution was satisfied that after their witnesses had been heard, they had demonstrated that the accused were in Turnbull's company on the day of the murder; that they had sold game as described by Turnbull; that the footprints had proved that Nichol at least had been at the murder scene; and that both of the accused had been seen spending large amounts of money in the days following the murder.

The defence called no witnesses, simply arguing that Turnbull's statement was unreliable and that there was no real evidence that proved beyond a reasonable doubt that the accused men were responsible for the crime.

The judge began his summing up by referring once more to Turnbull's statement, and was still concerned that he could not be questioned. The judge pointed to one discrepancy; Turnbull had said that the murder occurred within about 60 yards of Thompson first seeing the poachers, whereas the Crown's evidence regarding the footprints near to the murder scene suggested that it was in fact more than a mile from where the game watcher had first spotted the poachers, to where he was eventually killed. The judge believed this was of crucial importance, and told the jury:

> Just for a moment consider this matter. An ordinary accomplice is a very bad man to rely on at any time, but what is the state of the case when he is called? He is put in the witness box, you can see him, you hear what he says, and can observe his manner, but he is subject to cross-examination, and the effect of the questions upon him, may tell materially upon the jury. This accomplice you have never seen, but you know he has sworn falsely. How can you then put faith in his statement without having the opportunity of cross-examining him? I say, is it safe; is it reasonable to act upon such testimony?

The jury deliberated for a few moments where they sat, and returned not guilty verdicts. Hogg and Nichol left the court having been cleared of responsibility for the crime, and the murder of Thomas Davidson would remain officially unsolved.

FIVE

LAKELAND'S CONCEALED BABIES CASE

⊰ LAKELAND, 1877 ⊱

Forty-one-year-old Elizabeth Mary Louise Kirkbride opened a school for day pupils in Langwathby, which unfortunately failed, leaving her with little income. She fell into rent arrears as a result of which, solicitor's clerk George Haughton, accompanied by his close friend William Jameson, landlord of the Griffin Inn at Penrith, arrived at her home on Thursday 6 June 1876 to serve a distress warrant. An inventory of her belongings was taken and an auction was held the next day, at which enough of her furniture was sold to enable her to clear the rent arrears and her other debts.

When the auction had ended, Mrs Kirkbride advised Mr Jameson of her plans to move away from the area in the next few days, as she was going to live with two of her sons in Liverpool. She asked if she might store some of her boxes at the inn, which she promised would be collected once she had settled in her new home. The landlord agreed, and the next day Mrs Kirkbride paid local man Donald Robinson 1s to take the boxes in his cart to the Griffin. There were two boxes: a cask and a hamper, both of which were put in a spare room at the inn. Within a few days, Mr Jameson noticed an odd smell, but thought it emanated from the ferrets he kept in one of the upstairs rooms.

A few weeks later Mr Jameson received the following letter, which gave the address 21 Sutton Street, Tuebrook, Liverpool. It was not signed, but he correctly presumed it had been written by one of Mrs Kirkbride's sons:

Dear Sir,
Will you be kind enough to send the luggage by luggage train, with the exception of the hamper of china, which one of my brothers will call for on Tuesday next. If you could send them off tomorrow or Tuesday we would be very much obliged to you. I have enclosed directed envelope, if you will send me a line to say when they are sent off. Would you kindly

pack the bedding on the top of the large box, without the lid. My mother is very much obliged to you for your trouble, and will give you compensation if you will only say what she is in your debt.

Mr Jameson and his wife were too busy to comply with these requests, and a few days later a young man saying he was the son of Mrs Kirkbride called at the inn. Mr Jameson made it clear that he was far too busy to deal with the matter, nor was he prepared to bear the expense of sending the items to Liverpool, despite the promise of compensation. The young man left, saying he would make alternative arrangements, and although he returned once more, the items were not collected and remained at the inn.

At four o'clock on the afternoon of Thursday 25 January 1877, Isabelle Caruthers, who worked at the Griffin, noticed a strong smell in the room in which Mrs Kirkbride's property was stored. She informed Mrs Jameson, who opened one of the boxes. Inside were some old clothes and a smaller trunk, which she also opened. The stench was dreadful, and amidst the rags, wrapped in an old skirt, was what both horrified women recognised to be a baby's decomposed body.

The police were informed and Sergeant James Fraser arrived. He arranged for Dr Thomson to view the body, and, following a brief initial examination, he confirmed they were the remains of a baby who had been dead for some time.

An inquest was arranged for the following day, which was held at the Griffin Inn before the coroner, John Carrick. The members of the jury viewed the body, one of whom was

Elizabeth Kirkbride opened her school for day pupils in Langwathby. (Cumbria County Council)

HORRIBLE DISCOVERY NEAR LIVERPOOL.

At Tuebrook, one of the suburbs of Liverpool, a horrible discovery has just been made by the police. It appears that a woman named Kilbride recently came to live at Tuebrook from Penrith, Cumberland. Some days ago a box which she left there was found to contain the bodies of two children, and her apprehension on a charge of concealing the birth of these children led to a discovery of another box in her house in Tuebrook containing the bodies of three other children, all very much decomposed.

The discovery of the dead children led to widespread coverage in the press. (Author's collection)

not convinced that the remains were human, as he believed they were those of a monkey. The coroner conceded that as yet no post-mortem had been performed, and he asked Dr Thomson to perform one as the hearing proceeded.

The doctor confirmed that it was a human body, but it was in such an advanced stage of decomposition that he could not determine the sex. Nor could he say definitely if the child had lived after delivery, which he thought had been about six years earlier. Around the neck he found a piece of black silk, which was possibly a woman's garter, a strip of calico and a length of white cord, all of which had been tied and knotted so tightly that he could not force his finger between them and the body. They had caused a deep furrow around the neck, and he surmised that if the baby had lived, the ligatures could have been the cause of death.

The doctor concluded his evidence by suggesting that the baby had been delivered without the presence of a medically trained person, as, 'The umbilical cord had been rent asunder, and had not been tied.'

Having listened to the doctor's evidence, a jury member expressed the view that there were pieces of what looked like the remnants of a nightdress on the body, and if this was so, it indicated that the baby had been alive and had probably been strangled. The coroner, however, urged caution, stating that it could not be definitely proved that the pieces of cloth were those of a baby's nightdress. The jury accepted that it was not possible to reach a definite conclusion as to the cause of death, and returned an open verdict.

Later that evening, Sergeant Fraser placed the body in a coffin ready for burial. Having done so, he decided to examine the trunk in which it had been discovered once more. He removed some scraps of wallpaper, pieces of carpet, and a blanket, beneath which he found the body of another baby. It was wrapped in a bloodstained linen sheet, and appeared to be larger than the first body, and in a much more advanced state of decomposition.

Dr Thomson was again called upon to perform a post-mortem. He found the baby's chest and abdomen to have been crushed, and that the head had been almost severed. He did not believe that a knife had been used, as there were ligature marks around the neck, and although no cord was now present, he concluded that one must have been pulled so tightly that it had caused the deep neck wounds. The umbilical cord was tied appropriately, and the doctor calculated that the child, the sex of which he could not determine, had been dead for between six and seven years. Once more, he could not say whether or not it had lived after having been delivered.

The Penrith police knew that the trunk had been left at the inn by Mrs Kirkbride, and they also knew where she was living, as her address was given on the letter from her son to Mr and Mrs Jameson. A warrant was therefore issued for her arrest on suspicion of concealing the two births, and on Sunday night, Sergeant Robinson of the Kirkdale Division of the Lancashire County Police, arrived at her lodgings. The front door was opened by Mrs Kirkbride, whom he recognised from the description he had been given. Having explained the charges, he then placed her under arrest, but she claimed that there must be some mistake, as she knew nothing of such matters. She asked if she could leave a note for her sons, which the sergeant agreed to, but he insisted on seeing its contents. In it she advised them that she had been arrested on a warrant and was being taken to Penrith, but she would return in a few days. She asked the sergeant if they could leave the house as quietly as possible, to spare her the embarrassment of the other residents becoming aware that she was being arrested.

She was taken to the Old Swan police station, and on Monday morning a telegram was sent to the police at Penrith to advise them of her detention, and requesting that an officer be sent to collect her. However, within a few hours, further developments would mean that a transfer of the prisoner could not take place, for the time being at least.

That morning, the prisoner's son, John, entered his mother's rooms before leaving for work, and read her note. He presumed the warrant was in respect of an unpaid debt, and expected his mother to return to the lodgings in the near future. He went to work and returned at lunchtime, to be met by an angry Emma Oberti, the owner of 21 Sutton Street. She demanded to know why his mother had left without letting her know, and continued by accusing the missing woman of stealing one of her coats. John replied that his mother was not a thief, and offered a piece of cut glass as a surety until her return later in the week. Mrs Oberti refused this offer, and by then John too had become angry, and invited her to search the room. He also insisted upon opening his mother's boxes, to prove the coat was not hidden in one of them.

John forced the padlock of the first, and a strong smell was immediately evident, which he assumed was due to the old clothes contained in it. However, Mrs Oberti noticed what she thought was a small piece of human bone. She summoned the police, and the box and its contents were removed for further examination. They were taken to the West Derby Mortuary, where Dr Henry Pitts found the bodies of three babies piled on top of each other, each of which was wrapped in dirty rags. They had been in the box for a considerable length of time, and had been compressed by so much weight over the years that all of the remains were just two or three inches deep.

On top, he found the mummified body of a baby with a piece of rag tied tightly around the neck. Next, he removed the headless, mummified body of a second child; and beneath this he discovered the skeletal remains of a third child. He found it impossible to determine the sex of any of the bodies, nor could he be certain how long it had been since they died, other than that it was a number of years. He was unable to state whether or not they had lived after being delivered, and he could not provide a cause of death in respect of any of them.

As the bodies had been discovered in Liverpool it was necessary for an inquest to be held there, and later for Mrs Kirkbride to appear before the local magistrates. This took a few days, and she was eventually charged with concealing the births of the three children. It was decided that she should stand trial in the Lake District, for it was in that area that all of the alleged crimes appeared to have been committed.

While being held in the Old Swan cells, the prisoner made two statements to Inspector Walsh. The first was made when he charged her with the three additional offences, and she replied, 'Yes, they are all my children. I admit that I concealed them and neglected them, but I deny that I murdered any of them.'

The second statement was made later to the Inspector, and on this occasion she revealed more details, saying:

> I want to tell you the father of all the children I am here about. His name is Thomas Moss. He is the only man I had anything to do with in any way, and I think it is only right that he should be exposed, as it is entirely by his own person that I am placed as I am. He has always promised that he would make me his wife. Instead of doing so, when he was in a position, he married another.

Once he learnt that his name had been mentioned by Mrs Kirkbride, Thomas Moss, a wealthy grocer who lived in Askham, hired a solicitor to represent his interests. The solicitor was present at all subsequent hearings, and his client was not called upon to give evidence. His lawyer also took out an injunction preventing an enterprising Penrith photographer from selling images of the couple together.

THE DISCOVERY OF CHILDREN'S BODIES AT PENRITH AND LIVERPOOL.

On Saturday, at the County Magistrates' Court, Liverpool, before Messrs. R. Withers, A. Fenton, and G. W. Moss, Elizabeth Mary Louise Kirkbride, in whose box were recently found the dead bodies of three children, was brought up. The formal charge against the prisoner was that of having between the 4th June and the 29th ult. concealed the bodies of three of her illegitimate children in a box at No. 31, Sutton-street, Tuebrook, Liverpool.

Mrs Kirkbride's court appearance in Liverpool is reported. (Author's collection)

Askham, home of Thomas Moss, the alleged father of the dead children. (Cumbria County Council)

The accused's sons, John and William, were caused considerable distress by the accusations being made against their mother. They were also appalled by them, and co-operated fully with the police investigation. William revealed details of an incident six years earlier, when the family lived with their maternal grandmother in Helston. He had swept up some rubbish, which he took to the midden, in which he noticed a white bag tied up with string. Curious, he opened it, and wrapped in a petticoat was the body of a baby.

He threw the bag and its contents back into the midden, and although he did not mention the find to his mother, he did tell his grandmother and two visiting aunts. They warned him to forget what he had seen, and to never mention it again. The next day he was in the garden when he noticed an area of freshly disturbed earth. He removed a little soil and saw that it was a shallow grave, containing what he recognised as the body he had seen the day before.

On 1 February 1877, William revisited his childhood home at Helston, accompanied by Constable John Reed. They did not find a body in the garden, but they did discover several fragments of bone, which were later examined by Dr Taylor of Penrith and Dr Dinwoodie of Appleby. They concluded that the bones were not human, but in view of William's revelations, the police believed that there was sufficient circumstantial evidence to charge Mrs Kirkbride with a sixth offence of concealing a birth.

The Penrith police traced Mary Forsyth, who was working as a domestic servant in Burnley, but who, eleven years earlier, had been similarly employed by Mrs Kirkbride at the house in Helston. She recalled a Sunday morning when she saw her employer in bed with a child about one year old. She had not seen the child previously nor did she see it at any time afterwards. The child's identity could not be discovered, nor could a link be established to any of the bodies that had been found. Nevertheless, it demonstrated that a child other than her now adult children had been seen in her presence and whose whereabouts or fate could not be substantiated.

The decision having been made that the accused woman should stand trial in Penrith, it was necessary to make arrangements to take her there. Such was the level of public hostility directed towards her, it was recognised this would not be a straightforward exercise. There had already been an attempt to attack her at a hearing in Liverpool, and the police feared for her safety.

The task of escorting her was given to Superintendent Fowler, who arranged for barricades to be erected at Liverpool's Lime Street station to prevent a hostile crowd from reaching his prisoner. Nevertheless, a number of people did make it through to the platform from which their train was leaving, and it became necessary for a group of brave porters to push the crowd back from the carriage in which the Superintendent and his escort were sitting. The train left without a major incident occurring, but news having leaked out, crowds assembled at many of the stations on the route northwards. Some shouted abuse at her, and others could be heard making the unmistakable sounds of crying babies. Many Penrith residents had assembled to greet the train, and with Mrs Kirkbride leaning on his arm, the superintendent managed to pass through the hostile crowd to an omnibus, which took them to the police station, without her suffering any physical injuries.

Later in the week she appeared before the Penrith bench, and was committed to appear before the next assizes. By this time the Crown had decided, albeit reluctantly, that there was insufficient evidence to charge her with murder, as it had proved impossible to determine if any of the babies had been born alive; even if it had been possible to do so, a cause of death could not be established in any of the six cases.

So who was Mrs Kirkbride the most prolific serial killer in the land? She was the only child of respectable middle-class parents. Her father, John Hayton, had been a government surveyor in Liverpool, who, on his retirement, moved from Everton to Helston, where his daughter spent her formative years. Having married when she was quite young, Mrs Kirkbride was widowed in 1864, and was left with four children to raise alone. She returned to Helston to live in her mother's home, and opened a day school. In 1876, she and her mother moved to Langwathby, where the older woman died two weeks later. She opened another school, but this was not a success. She had managed to attract just one pupil and it was then that she fell into rent arrears, which was to set in motion the events leading to the children's bodies being discovered.

She appeared before the Westmorland Assizes in late February 1877, before Mr Justice Manisty. She entered the dock wearing a black veil, which the judge ordered to be removed. She faced three charges, all of which related to the concealment of the births of children, the first being at Helston, despite a body not having been discovered, secondly in a box found at Penrith, and thirdly in a box discovered at Tuebrook. The accused was not legally represented, and pleaded guilty to all three matters.

Mrs Kirkbride appeared at a number of hearings before coroners and magistrates in Penrith and Liverpool, and at all a sense of frustration could be discerned from the statements made by officials and jury members that it had not been possible to charge her with more serious offences. In passing sentence, the judge echoed these sentiments, and he told her that she was fortunate not to be facing murder charges. He pointed particularly to the cases in which ligatures had been discovered, or it had been strongly suspected that one had been used, but it had been removed. Clearly, there were many loose ends in this case; for instance, had she murdered all of the children? Were there even more dead babies? Did she act alone, or was she perhaps coerced into committing the crimes? These and other questions were to remain unanswered.

The judge sentenced her to nine months imprisonment on each count, and the sentences were to run consecutively. This meant she would serve a total of twenty-seven months, which many believed was far too short a sentence.

SIX

THE HINDPOOL TRAGEDY

⊰ HINDPOOL, 1878 ⊱

Number 6 Tay Street, Hindpool, a tenement known as Scotch Building, comprised six flats; A and B were located at ground level, C and D were on the first floor, and E and F on the top floor. There was a common yard and a shared entrance leading from the street, which was usually kept locked, but for which all the tenants held keys.

On Friday 25 October 1878, labourer Samuel Edgar, who lived in 6C, was putting up a washing line in the yard. He climbed on to the windowsill at the rear of 6A to fasten one end of the line to a hook on the wall, and looking into the room he saw the body of a woman lying on the floor. He went in search of a police officer and returned to the scene with Constable Sanderson. They found the door to 6A locked, but Samuel's key opened it, and he identified the body as that of his neighbour, Ann McGuinneas.

The flat comprised two sparsely furnished, filthy rooms, and the constable noticed a few items of men's and women's clothing, which were little more than rags. In one corner there was a heap of rotting food, and on the table he noticed a pan containing a cow's head immersed in water, ready for boiling. Although not certain of the cause of death, there was a great deal of blood, and assuming she had been stabbed, the constable made a preliminary examination of the knives at the scene. However, there was no trace of blood on any of them, and none seemed to be sharp enough to have been used as a weapon.

The police established that the dead woman lived at the address with her husband, William, who could not be traced. The couple, who were both in their mid-thirties, had been married for a number of years, and had a nine-year-old son and a younger daughter, who were staying with relatives. William and Ann were poor and had been living an itinerant existence for much of their married life. They had visited the Hindpool area occasionally over the years, and worked at whatever jobs they could find. They had been living in the Scotch Building for the previous three weeks, and Ann had found employment in a local factory, and her husband was employed as a labourer at Carnforth railway station. He stayed there during the week, but travelled home at the weekend.

THE MURDER AT BARROW.

The adjourned inquest on the body of Ann M'Guinness, who is alleged to have been murdered at Barrow on the 19th October by her husband, William M'Guinness, was held last evening.—Joseph Fairclough, a railway porter at Carnforth, gave evidence to the effect that M'Guinness told him at Carnforth on the 21st of October that he had murdered his wife—that he had kicked her across the floor, and left her for dead. Witness told several persons what M'Guinness had said, but it was not believed, and no notice was taken of it. Several neighbours gave evidence to the effect that they heard screams on the night of the murder, but did not think anything was wrong.—Dr. Murray, who had made a *post-mortem* examination of the body, said death had resulted from a stab wound in the left thigh, by which the main artery was severed.—Inspector Barlow, of the local police force, stated that M'Guinness a few days before the murder threatened in his presence "what he would do," for his wife. M'Guinness complained that his wife was unfaithful to him, and that she pawned his clothes.—A verdict of wilful murder was returned.—A telegram reached Barrow last night stating that a man answering the description of M'Guinness had been apprehended in the West Riding of Yorkshire. M'Guinness has been traced from Lancaster to Garstang, Preston, and Todmorden into Yorkshire.

The murder of Ann McGuineas is reported, together with news of her husband's disappearance. (Author's collection)

The relationship was known to be an unhappy one. She was a decent and sober woman, who was a loving mother and faithful wife, whereas he was a drunkard who was often violent towards Ann. He regularly accused her of being unfaithful, for in common with other cowardly men who beat their wives, he needed to fabricate a reason in his own mind to justify to himself his brutality towards her.

The last occasion they had been seen together was on the previous Saturday night, 19 October, when at ten o'clock labourer John Douglas, who lived on Hindpool Road and knew the couple, met them in the Hartington Hotel. After one drink the three of them went to the Devonshire Hotel for one more, before starting for home shortly after ten thirty.

John told the police that William was so drunk that he was incapable of walking unaided, and was having to lean on Ann for support. He accused her of being unfaithful, and called her a whore. He threatened to kill her, but John thought that Ann, whom he believed must have heard similar threats from her husband many times in the past, did not seem unduly concerned. John parted from the couple when they reached the post office, and he did not see them again.

Mary Wright, who lived at 6F, had borrowed Ann's key to the street entrance to the tenement earlier that evening. They arranged that Mary would admit her when she returned later that night. Mary did so, and she too saw that Ann was sober, unlike her husband who was very drunk. She watched as they entered their flat, and a few minutes later she heard a cry of 'Murder!' However, she could not be certain that it came from 6A and took no further action. Another neighbour, Mary Stephenson, who lived next door to William and Ann at 6B, did not see them return to the building but heard two screams coming from their flat at a few minutes before eleven o'clock. This was not an unusual occurrence in the tenement, and she thought no more of it.

William McGuinneas had not been seen in Hindpool since the previous Saturday night, but on the following Monday morning he had reported for work at Carnforth. He later spoke with George Fairclough, a porter, who realised that his workmate was drunk, and when he asked how he was, McGuinneas replied, 'First rate. Give me your hand, I'm going away.' He told the porter that he was not in trouble at work, but that he had left his wife for dead at home. Later that afternoon, George saw McGuinneas enter the third-class carriage of a train about to leave for Catterall.

The inquest into Ann's death took place on Saturday 26 October, before the coroner Mr J. Poole. The jury first of all examined the body, before hearing the evidence of Samuel Edgar, John Douglas, Mary White, Mary Stephenson, Constable Sanderson and Joseph Fairclough. Inspector Barlow also gave evidence at the hearing, that on Wednesday 16 October a drunken McGuinneas had arrived at the local police station, where he had complained that while he had been working away from home, his wife had pawned some of his clothing. He demanded that the police take action against her, but on being informed that it was not a police matter, he swore that he would kill her. The Inspector, believing this to be an empty threat, allowed him to leave. After hearing the evidence of these witnesses the coroner adjourned the hearing until the following Thursday, to await the results of a post-mortem.

The post-mortem was performed by Dr Murray the same afternoon, and he gave details of his findings at the adjourned hearing. He had discovered Ann lying in the room, which was smeared in blood, and found her to be a well-nourished woman. From the state of decomposition he believed that she had been dead between six and ten days. There were bruises to her head, but these were old injuries and not a factor in her death. There was darkness about the head but this was post-mortem lividity. The lower part of her body, together with the black dress she was wearing, her stockings and clogs, were covered with blood. On a level with her left thigh there was a hole which passed through several layers of her clothing, and corresponding with this, at the front of her left thigh, was a gaping wound more than three inches long, two inches wide and several inches deep. The principal artery of the leg and a large vein had been severed.

The wound had been caused by a sharp implement, probably a knife, which had been struck from below in an upward direction. Dr Murray concluded that very great force had been necessary, and although the injury could possibly have been self-inflicted he doubted this was the case, as he did not think Ann would have been strong enough to have performed such an act. It was also unlikely that the wound could have been caused by accidentally falling on to a knife. He concluded that she had bled to death, but he had been shown no weapon capable of inflicting such an injury at the scene.

In his summing up, the coroner highlighted the threats the absent McGuinneas had made against his wife in the presence of Inspector Barlow, and those he had uttered on the Saturday night after his drinking bout. Given the evidence that had been heard, Mr Poole could see no alternative explanation other than that Ann had been wilfully murdered by her husband. The jury took just a few minutes to reach their verdict, agreeing with the coroner, and in his absence, McGuinneas was committed to stand trial at Lancaster Assizes.

However, the jury was not finished, for the foreman, John Sansom, referring to the Scotch Building, said, 'I think the property is in a most disgraceful state and the owners ought to have their attention drawn to it. I think the owner ought to take charge of the public passages and keep them clean.' James Swindlehurst, a jury member, went further in his criticism, saying, 'There might be a dozen murders committed in such places as this. They stink with filth, and it is a wonder a murder was ever found out.'

The inquest having been concluded, it was now possible to release Ann's body for burial. She was taken from the mortuary and interred in the Roman Catholic section of the public cemetery. Revd Gordon officiated, and several of her friends gathered to pay their respects.

Meanwhile, a number of men suspected of being McGuinneas were detained in error in various parts of the country, but he managed to evade the police for more than a month. The Home Secretary agreed to offer a reward of £100, which was matched by the local justices, which meant that there was a total reward of £200 for his capture.

In view of his background, it was believed McGuinneas might have travelled to Ireland, and this proved to be the case, for that was where he was captured. On 21 October, after leaving Carnforth, he had travelled by train to Catterall, where he spent the night, before making his way to Hollyhead the following day. From there he took a ferry to Ireland and headed for Drogheda, his birthplace. He stayed with his mother for a few days before travelling to Dublin, where he found employment at the city's terminus of the new Drogheda railway, using the name William McGlaughlin. However, staff became suspicious for he matched the description given of the Hindpool fugitive in the reward notice, and the local police were contacted. He was detained and the mainland police informed.

Sergeant Baxendale, who knew McGuinneas, was sent to confirm the identity of the detained man. He recognised him immediately and charged him with the murder of his wife. McGuinneas replied, 'I deny it. I know nothing about it.' However, Constable Burton was dispatched from Barrow with a warrant, and the prisoner and the two officers acting as his escort arrived in Barrow on the night of Thursday 28 November.

McGuinneas appeared before the local magistrates the following morning, providing him with the opportunity of cross-examining the witnesses, which had not been possible at the inquest as he had been on the run when it was held. John Douglas, Mary White and Mary Stephenson repeated the evidence they gave before the coroner. The prisoner questioned them all at length, and made much of the fact that no one had actually seen the murder committed.

Nevertheless, two new and crucially important witnesses gave evidence which had not been heard at the inquest. Sylvester Bowman testified that on 6 November he was helping to clear the flat in which Ann had met her death, and concealed in a pile of flock he found a black-hafted knife, which he had handed to the police.

ARREST OF A MURDERER.

William M'Guinneas, aged 35, who murdered his wife at Barrow-in-Furness five weeks ago, and who has escaped justice up to the present time, has been apprehended at Dublin, where Sergent Baxendale, of the Barrow police force, has identified him It is stated that M'Guinneas has been an inmate of a hospital for three weeks. A medical student will receive the reward of £200 which was offered.

Confirmation that McGuinneas had been arrested in Dublin and that the reward had been claimed by a medical student. (Author's collection)

Now in possession of the knife, the police visited a number of local shops and discovered that McGuinneas had bought a white-hafted knife at Bolton's Ironmongers in late September. Shop assistant Robert Bond testified that at 6.30 p.m. on Saturday 19 October, a few hours before he allegedly murdered Ann, the accused had entered the shop and demanded to change the knife. He claimed it was blunt and he was unable to cut meat with it. It was agreed that he would pay an additional eleven pence and was provided with the much sharper black-hafted knife, later discovered by Sylvester Bowman, and which the prosecution alleged was the murder weapon. Having heard all of the evidence, the magistrates had no hesitation in committing McGuinneas to stand trial for wilful murder.

His trial took place at Lancaster Castle on Friday 17 January 1879 before Lord Justice Thesiger, and the prosecution was undertaken by Mr Baldwin and Mr Tomlinson. The defendant had been unable to afford to pay for a lawyer, and the judge directed that the Honourable A.D. Elliott should represent him.

The prosecution relied on the evidence provided by the witnesses who had testified at the preliminary hearings. The defence was based largely on the fact that all of the evidence was circumstantial, as nobody had seen the murder take place, and no evidence had been provided to show how the fatal blow was struck or by whom. Furthermore, it was argued that the jury should dismiss the threats he had made in front of witnesses, as he had done so regularly for many years, and on the night of the murder, Ann had not seemed particularly worried when she had heard them made against her. The defence concluded by suggesting that the wound could have been self-inflicted or might possibly have been caused accidentally after she had fallen on the knife.

In his summing up, the judge advised the jury that most trials, including those involving a charge of murder, were decided upon by circumstantial evidence. There was seldom a witness to such a crime, nor was there usually any reliable scientific evidence. As for the defence's claims that the wound could have been self-inflicted or been caused accidentally, the judge asked the jury to consider why, if either of these scenarios was correct, the knife was not found close to the body, as it had clearly been moved and hidden in the flock. Ann could not have done this, and if the accused had been present why would he want to hide the knife, which, the judge reminded the jury, he had exchanged just hours before the death of his wife, having made it clear in doing so that he wanted a much sharper blade. It might be thought that for a murderer to hide the weapon used in the crime at the scene was foolish behaviour. It would, after all, make more sense to move it far away to reduce the risk of it being found. However, the accused had been drinking heavily and his judgement therefore impaired, although this could not be used as a reason to reduce the charge to that of manslaughter.

Lord Justice Thesiger believed that the threat to kill his wife, made in the presence of Inspector Barlow a few nights before her death, was of crucial importance. It proved McGuinneas was very angry with Ann for allegedly pawning some of his belongings, and that he was still angry with her is evident from his behaviour towards her immediately before he allegedly murdered her on the Saturday night, when he was again heard to threaten to kill her.

The jury retired for twenty minutes before returning with a guilty verdict. The judge placed a black cap on his head and sentenced McGuinneas to death. There would be no petition raised by friends or family seeking a reprieve, and his execution was arranged for 8 a.m. on 11 February at Lancaster Castle.

The condemned man was a Catholic, and he spent a great deal of his time in the condemned cell in discussion and prayer with Father Walsh. McGuinneas was concerned for the futures of his son and daughter, who were now living with his mother in Drogheda. He seemed much reassured after receiving a letter from her saying that both would be raised by her, and a local miller, for whom the condemned's father had once worked, had promised to take the boy on and teach him the trade.

THE BARROW MURDERER.

William M'Guinness, who on Tuesday was sentenced to death at Lancaster Assizes, displays a stolid indifference to the position in which he is now placed. After the trial he was very anxious to know what had become of the money realised by the sale of his furniture, and what had been done with the money due to his wife at the Barrow Flax and Jute Works. He was informed that the former had been taken by the landlord for rent due, and the Board of Guardians, who buried his wife, had taken the latter. The condemned man has a son nine years of age and a daughter twelve years old. The execution is fixed to take place at Lancaster on the 11th of February.

Following his conviction and being sentenced to death, McGuinneas was told what had become of the money raised from the sale of his belongings and his wife's wages. (Author's collection)

EXECUTION AT LANCASTER.

This morning at eight o'clock, William McGuiness, labourer, convicted at the last Lancaster Assizes, for the murder of his wife at Barrow, was executed within the walls of Lancaster Castle. Marwood was the executioner. The hoisting of the black flag over the Gateway Tower four minutes afterwards announced the fact to the outside public. The culprit was not visited by any relations or friends. After his condemnation he has never denied that he killed his wife, but declared he never intended doing so. By order of the prison authorities, the representatives of the press were excluded from witnessing the execution, none but officials being present, who were very reticent about giving information regarding the execution.

Above: *News of the execution. (Author's collection)*

Left: *William Marwood, the hangman. (Author's collection)*

The executioner, William Marwood, arrived at Lancaster Castle at 5 p.m. on the eve of the hanging, having spent the day travelling from Worcester, where he had hanged a man that morning. The gallows had been erected in the castle yard to Marwood's specifications. The platform was reached by walking up a small flight of steps, and once McGuinneas was standing on the trap, a handle was turned and two trapdoors opened, through which he would fall. All of the woodwork was padded so there would be no loud crashing noise. The noose was suspended from a beam, and a hole was dug in the ground beneath to accommodate the drop of 8ft 6in.

The governor of Lancaster Castle had announced that no journalists would be allowed to witness the hanging, nor attend the inquest, which was also to be held in the castle. A deputation of press representatives arrived at the castle gates on the morning of the execution, but they were refused admission. By 7.30 a.m. a crowd of approximately 600 had gathered outside the gates, and thirty minutes later they watched as the black flag was raised, signifying that the execution had taken place. In accordance with custom, the businesses and houses around the castle kept their blinds and shutters closed as a mark of respect for the executed man, until 9 a.m., when his body was cut down.

It was later reported by sources within the castle that McGuinneas, fully resigned to his fate, had slept well and had eaten a light breakfast after waking up. He spent some time in prayer with Father Walsh, and walked with great composure to his death. The inquest was held later that morning before the coroner, Mr Holden, and the jury found that he had been killed lawfully of a broken neck.

SEVEN

THE MURDER OF CONSTABLE BYRNE

⇥ PLUMPTON, 1885 ⇤

Tuesday 27 October 1885 was the opening day of the Longtown coursing meeting, and many visitors flocked to the district. Therefore, the arrival of three strangers at Gretna railway station on the Carlisle train attracted no attention. Each of the men carried a suitcase, which they left with the stationmaster, saying they would collect them later.

However, these were no ordinary visitors, for they were three notorious London criminals; forty-five-year-old Anthony Benjamin Rudge, alias William Walsh and William Fennell; John Martin, alias John White, aged thirty-six; and twenty-nine-year-old James Baker. The expanding railway system meant that professional villains such as these could now travel easily to parts of the country where they were not known, commit their crimes, and flee the area in the same manner. However, the crimes these men committed during the next few days would ensure that their names, and more importantly those of the heroic local men involved in their capture, would long be remembered throughout the Lake District.

The following day, Baker returned to the station and took one of the suitcases to the Graham Arms Inn, where he and his companions had spent the night. David Johnstone, the landlady's son-in-law, watched as Baker took the case into a side room and took out one of the many keys it contained. The key was held up to the open fire before an attempt was made to insert it into a mechanism, which had also been taken out the bag. The men seemed dissatisfied, and Baker dipped the key into a glass of rum before again trying it in the mechanism. Apparently satisfied, the key was pocketed, and the suitcase locked. Baker returned with it to the station and arranged for the three bags to be taken to the left luggage office at Carlisle, where he said they would be collected in the near future by A. Smith.

The men set off walking in the direction of Longtown, and Mary Richardson, a field worker raking thorns at the side of the road, and carter William Atkinson, later identified them as having enquired about the habits and whereabouts of Sir Frederick Graham, owner of the nearby Netherby Hall.

At eight o'clock that evening, Margaret Watson, head housemaid at Netherby Hall, turned the handle of Lady Hermione Graham's bedroom, and to her surprise found it to be locked. She knew her mistress was dining with her husband Sir Frederick downstairs, and was immediately concerned, as the door was always kept unlocked. She hammered on the door and shouted into the room, demanding to know who was there, but was met with silence.

Margaret raised the alarm, and the butler, two maids and John Plenderleith, Sir Frederick's valet, were soon at her side. They were unable to open the door, and the valet rushed downstairs and into the garden. He found a ladder, which he carried to a spot beneath the bedroom, climbed to the window and entered the room, which was now empty. He opened the door to the others, and Lady Hermione discovered her jewellery case had been forced open and several items, later valued at £250, were missing. These included a pair of eardrops and three diamond stars.

The police were informed and Superintendent Sempill was put in charge of investigating the burglary. Within two hours, all of the police in the district had been alerted. It was thought that those responsible for the crime would probably head for Carlisle, and Sergeant John Roche was ordered to call at the Kingstown police house of Constable Jacob Johnstone, which was eight miles from Netherby Hall, and two miles from Carlisle. The two officers were to keep a watch out for any suspicious characters who might pass through the village.

The sergeant arrived at Kingstown at eleven o'clock, and his colleague had just opened the door to him when the officers saw a group of men, all of whom were strangers, approaching them. These were Baker, Rudge and Martin, and a fourth man, more of whom will be heard later. Sergeant Roche challenged them, and they replied that they were visiting the area for the coursing. The sergeant opened his top coat to reveal his police uniform, and ordered them into the police house to be searched.

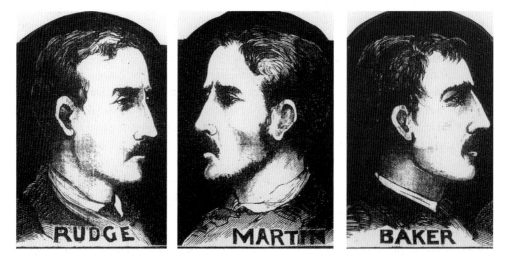

Left: *Anthony Benjamin Rudge.* Centre: *John Martin.* Right: *James Baker. (*Illustrated Police News)

The Graham Arms. (Cumbria County Council)

However, Baker shouted, 'I'll give you police officer', and, pulling a jemmy from his pocket, he lunged at the sergeant, hitting him on the head. The sergeant did not fall to the ground, but instead took out his truncheon, with which he hit Baker, causing him to stagger. It was then that the sergeant saw Rudge and Martin aiming revolvers at him, and heard two shots. He felt a bullet enter his arm, and he fell to the ground, after which the four men ran off. Despite his wound, the sergeant ordered Constable Johnstone to leave him and follow the four men.

Sergeant Roche managed to rise to his feet, intending to join in the chase, but before he could do so there was another shot, followed by the voice of Constable Johnstone crying out, 'I am shot! I am shot!' The sergeant arranged for his wounded colleague to be looked after by villagers, before setting off for Carlisle, where he helped to search the railway station for the gang.

The shot that wounded Constable Johnstone had also been heard by Sergeant Hadley, who was standing several hundred yards away. He ran to the houses of nurseryman Thomas Armstrong and auctioneer George Hetherington, telling them to bring their guns. Neither man possessed a weapon, but they had no hesitation in joining the sergeant, and it was only a matter of a few minutes before they encountered the four men. Sergeant Hadley demanded to know their business and was told that they had been attacked by a gang a few minutes earlier. Not satisfied with this answer, the sergeant grabbed one of them by his coat collar, but the man produced a revolver from his pocket. The other men threatened the officer and his two companions, which led Mr Armstrong to urge the officer, 'Leave go Hadley, and let us get out of this as quickly as possible.' Sergeant Hadley had little option but to loosen his grip as he and his civilian companions were unarmed, and reluctantly he let the man go free.

Left: *The burglary at Netherby Hall and the shootings of Sergeant Roche and Constable Johnstone at Kingstown. (*Illustrated Police News*)*

Below: *Carlisle station. (Author's collection)*

The men hurried away and were later seen walking along the railway line close to Carlisle by John Strong, the level crossing keeper at Shaddongate. He informed Constable Christopher Fortune, who arrived at the crossing a few minutes later. The officer caught up with the gang and called out to them, 'Hello chaps, what's up here at this time of the morning?' Without warning, the men rushed him and gave him a severe beating. He was unconscious for several minutes, but eventually found his way to a nearby signal box where Thomas Evans was on duty. So severe had the beating been that when he first saw him, the signalman thought that the officer had been hit by a train. There were now three badly injured police officers requiring medical attention.

At twenty minutes past midnight, Dr Henry Lediard of the Cumberland Infirmary arrived to treat Constable Johnstone's wound. He removed a bullet which had entered his body four inches below the right nipple, and which had passed through his liver. The wounded officer was to remain in danger for some time, but fortunately made a full recovery, and for his conduct that night was promoted to the rank of sergeant.

Two hours later, the doctor arrived at the home of Sergeant Roche, and removed a bullet from a wound to the upper arm, which had lodged very close to a major artery. However, he would also make a full recovery, and he was promoted to Inspector in recognition of the courage and leadership that he too had shown that night.

Robert Walker, the police surgeon, treated Constable Fortune and found nineteen head injuries resulting from a serious beating by a number of heavy blunt instruments. He was suffering from shock, and the doctor would continue to treat him for several weeks. He came close to losing his life, but he too survived the ordeal.

Nothing was seen of the wanted men until 5 p.m., when Constable Joseph Byrne visited Calthwaite railway station to warn the stationmaster, John Hays, and porter, William Milburn, to be on the look out for the gang. Three hours later Rudge, Martin and Baker arrived and enquired about trains to London and Carlisle. They left after being told that there were no trains to those destinations, and Mr Hays immediately sent telegrams to Carlisle, Penrith, Southwaite and Plumpton stations.

Within a short time of the message being received at Plumpton, a lone stranger approached the stationmaster, William Gornall, asking for a timetable. Mr Gornall found his behaviour suspicious, as the man attempted to cover as much of his face as possible with his collar and hat. Furthermore, rather than read the timetable by the bright light of the waiting room, he took it outside to read by the much dimmer light on the platform. Having discovered that there would be no train to London until the following morning, the man left.

Brothers Thomas and William Lowthian arrived at the station a few minutes later, and the stationmaster told them of his visitor. The brothers said that they had seen the man meet two other strangers a short distance from the station, and it was agreed that the brothers would call on Constable Byrne to advise him of these events. The constable was told that they had walked towards the centre of the village, and he set off in the same direction. He met Thomas Simpson, who told the officer that he had spoken with the men, who had wanted to know where the nearest public house was. He had directed them to the Pack Horse Inn, and it was a little after eight thirty that the constable left Thomas and walked towards the inn. Meanwhile, the three men had drunk two glasses of ale at the Pack Horse, and left the inn with a pint of rum and some bread and cheese.

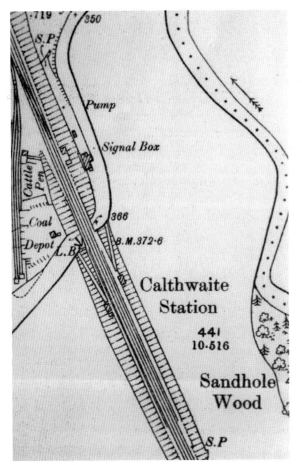

Calthwaite station. (Cumbria County Coucil)

It was only a very short time after they had left that a single gunshot was heard throughout the village. It seemed particularly loud to Revd H.M. Kennedy, his housekeeper Elizabeth Irving and her daughter Margaret, in the vicarage, and on checking his clock, the vicar noted that it was eight thirty-four.

Ninety minutes later, Thomas Lowthian left the Pack Horse, and after walking a short distance he noticed a pool of blood in the road, opposite the vicarage. He also heard groaning noises coming from behind a nearby wall, but when he looked over it into the field it was too dark for him to see anything. He ran back to the inn for assistance and returned with a lantern and three other men.

In the field they discovered the badly wounded Constable Byrne, who was unable to speak. They carried him on a door to the inn, where he was examined by medical student William Matthews, who found a severe head wound. The officer was clearly beyond help, and died without regaining consciousness at one o'clock in the morning.

At about this time, Constable James Patterson was on duty at Thacka Bridge, a quarter of a mile from Penrith, when he noticed three men walking along the railway track in the direction of the town. He ran to Penrith station to alert his colleagues, and an extensive but unsuccessful search was made. The men had gone to the sidings from which a goods train heading south was pulling away. They jumped into a wagon, but as they did so they were seen by the guard, Christopher Gaddes, who was convinced they must be the Netherby Hall burglars. As the train passed Keswick Junction, he shouted to the signalman but could not make himself heard. He therefore wrote a note, which read: 'Write to the stationmaster at Tebay to be prepared to look after three men I have on the train.' He threw it out at Shap but saw that it had not been noticed by his colleagues, and so he wrote a similar note, and at Shap Summit threw it into the cab of a stationery engine, the driver of which shouted that he had caught it.

The train pulled into Tebay at 11.40 p.m., but the police had not yet arrived. However, several railwaymen had assembled on the platform and were awaiting the train's arrival, having armed themselves with a variety of iron bars and wooden sticks. The hiding place of the three men was discovered, and they attempted to escape. However, Martin was hit on the head by foremen George Beatty, forcing him to the ground. As he struggled to his feet, Martin exclaimed, 'What do you mean? I am one of the men in search of the robbers!' In response, the foreman hit him on the head once again and he was tied up by engine driver William Parker. Rudge fared no better, and he was caught as he clambered down an embankment. He threatened his pursuers with a revolver, but they were not deterred and

*The murder of Constable Byrne. (*Illustrated Police News*)*

69

Shap Summit. (Cumbria County Council)

he was brought down by a blow from a heavy iron bar by messenger John Wills. Having been overpowered and disarmed, Martin and Rudge were tied to a post as they awaited the arrival of the police, who took the captured men to Carlisle on a goods train two hours later. Baker avoided capture at Tebay, and disappeared into the darkness. However, he was seen jumping into the wagon of another goods train heading south by its driver, Thomas Matley.

The driver stopped the train at Oxenholme, where he made a search of the wagons, but the man could not be found. However, as the train was pulling out of the station, he saw the man emerge from behind a hedge and clamber once again into a wagon. He stopped the train at Carnforth and made another unsuccessful search, but the game of cat and mouse continued, for as the train was leaving the platform, he watched as the man came out of the shadows and jump onto the train. Later, the train stopped at Lancaster, where Thomas saw the man leap out of a wagon and run away.

It was now 2.15 a.m., and by chance the London express was standing at another platform. The guard, Henry Cooper, noticed Baker attempting to board the train, and demanded that he produce his ticket. When he failed to do so, the guard grabbed him and shouted, 'You are the man that's wanted.' Baker attempted to struggle free but could not do so, as by now three porters had arrived to help their colleague overpower him. He was detained at the station until the police arrived later that morning to take him to Carlisle, where he was reunited with Rudge and Martin.

The three men were charged with a catalogue of crimes by Superintendent Sempill, who offered them the opportunity of giving accounts of their movements over the previous few days. Rudge declined to make any statement, but Martin and Baker did so. Martin explained that he had travelled to the area from his home in Edinburgh, and had not known either of the two other men until meeting Rudge the previous night in a public house. He insisted that he knew nothing of the events in Longtown, Kingstown or Plumpton. Baker told the Superintendent that he had a business in Bethnal Green, and had arrived alone at Longtown on Tuesday, where he spent the night. On Wednesday he had travelled to Newcastle-upon-Tyne, where he visited a brothel, and he had left Carlisle by passenger train the previous evening.

The police had three men in custody, but several witnesses had reported the presence of a fourth man on Wednesday night. A well-known criminal, William Baker, who had served eighteen months for his involvement in the theft of the jewels of the Duke of Montrose some years earlier, had been seen at the Longtown coursing meeting. He was suspected of being the fourth man and was arrested in Manchester. He was taken to Carlisle for questioning, where he denied most vehemently being the fourth member of the gang. He insisted that he had left Carlisle by train on Wednesday night at 8.30 p.m., arriving in Manchester four hours later. Sergeant Roche and Mr Hetherington, both of whom had seen the fourth man, failed to identify him, and Carlisle's Chief Constable Dunne had to hand him his train fare back to Manchester.

The courage displayed by the wounded police officers and the murdered constable led inevitably to the issue of arming the police as a matter of routine being raised. One correspondent, whose letter was published in the *Carlisle Patriot*, undoubtedly represented the views of many when he wrote:

Tebay station. (Cumbria County Council)

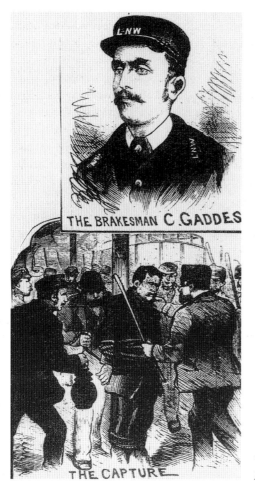

THE BRAKESMAN C. GADDES

THE CAPTURE

The guard, Christopher Gaddes and the capture of Martin and Rudge. (Illustrated Police News)

Sir, It is to be hoped that the terrible murder at Plumpton, and the attempted murders at Kingstown and Carlisle, will nerve up our authorities to admit the absolute necessity of supplying the police with the necessary firearms to cope on equal terms with such ruffians as they go about the country plundering and murdering right and left. I contend Sir, that if such brutes, for they are nothing else, knew that the police were not only armed with the law but with the very best revolvers, they would give our very much abused officers a wide berth; and we would cease to hear of such robberies and the inevitable subsequent murder or attempted murder of some plucky policeman who tried to effect a capture. Is it fair to ask the police to face such desperadoes, who are armed to the teeth, with nothing better than an ordinary old-fashioned stick? Timorous sentimentalists may say, 'Oh, but the police might lose their heads and shoot some innocent person.' Is it likely? The policeman would not draw his revolver until he was threatened himself, and then only in self-defence, and in a strict execution of his duty. I am fully persuaded that there would seldom or never be any need for the use of their firearms, because the murderous class are the greatest cowards, and as soon as they knew that they had no advantage over the police, murders like these would cease, just as garrotting ceased as soon as the cowards got a taste of the 'cat.' [This refers to the garrotting panic of the 1850s and 1860s, which was ended, so it was argued, by the introduction of severe penalties, including lengthy prison sentences and corporal punishment.] Perhaps it might be necessary to shoot two or three of these gentry, the same as we shoot a mad dog or a tyke we catch worrying sheep or lambs. This would, in my humble opinion, be enough to put a stop to the whole system as at present carried out by the disciples of Peace. [This refers to Charlie Peace, a notorious Victorian murderer, hanged at Leeds, who, on the eve of his execution, confessed to murdering a police constable in Manchester some years earlier.] There have already been more than sufficient victims to satisfy all but nervous old women that it is high time we armed our police.

Before closing this letter I respectfully suggest that a country subscription, for it is a national matter, should be opened to provide for the widow and children of the murdered policeman at Plumpton, who died in the execution of his duty, as bravely as any warrior ever yielded up his life's blood in the hardest contested field of glory, and his belongings [*sic*] ought to be placed beyond the fear of needing bread. Something also should be done for Roche, Johnstone and Fortune, and the guard must not be forgotten. To this fund I will give £1.

REVOLVER, Carlisle, October 31st 1885.

The identities and criminal careers of the three arrested men became known after their descriptions had been circulated to other police forces throughout the country. Baker had been a burglar since his youth, and was a ticket of leave man, following his release from a sentence of five years penal servitude, which had been imposed for a robbery at Greenwich. Rudge was also a ticket of leave man following his release from a sentence of five years penal servitude. Previously he had served ten years for robbery and the attempted murders of two police officers.

The Essex force was particularly interested in Martin, who was suspected of being involved in the murder of one of their officers earlier in the year. Inspector Simmons had been shot dead as he attempted to arrest three men seen committing a robbery. One man, James Lee, had been hanged for the crime at Chelmsford Gaol in May, but the other two men were still at large. Detective Sergeant Rolfe had been threatened with a revolver by one of them, and he travelled north together with Chief Inspector Shore to see if Martin was indeed one of the wanted men. At Carlisle, the Detective Sergeant identified the prisoner as the man who had shot at him, and murdered the Inspector.

Following the visit by the two southern police officers, Martin was heard to say to Rudge, 'I suppose I shall be done for the Romford murder now and for putting a squib up to Rolfe's nose.'

Information from other police forces suggested that the three men had been in the north of England and Scotland for several weeks, and had committed a number of other crimes during their stay. In the early hours of the morning, two weeks previously, the safe from Crookstown railway station had been taken and forced opened in a field, and £3 had been taken from it. An hour or so later the safe was removed from Cardonald station, and when later found; it had been forced open and £3 18s was missing. The burglars were seen by two Lanarkshire police officers who were shot at when they attempted to arrest them. The two officers travelled to Carlisle, where they identified Rudge and Martin as the two men they had encountered and who had shot at them.

*The murder scene and incidents associated with the crime. (*Illustrated Police News*)*

On 9 October 1885, Newton Hall, near Corbridge in Northumberland had been burgled, and an attempt made to remove valuable jewels. However, three men were interrupted by several dinner guests, who had been alerted by suspicious noises. These witnesses identified Baker and Rudge as two of those seen running across the lawn as they fled the scene.

The coroner, John Carrick, opened the inquest into the murdered officer's death at the Pack Horse on Friday 6 November. William Matthews was the first to give evidence, and he described the unsuccessful attempt to save Byrne due to the seriousness of his injury.

Dr Tristram Montgomery gave details of the post-mortem examination, which he had performed at the inn. The bullet had entered at the left eyebrow and the exit wound was one inch behind the left ear. The bullet had caused massive brain damage, and he would have become unconscious immediately. Either of the two revolvers recovered from the accused could have been the weapon responsible.

Dr Montgomery continued by describing extensive bruising to the deceased's right arm, between the wrist and shoulder, and bruising to his left wrist. This led the doctor to conclude that two men had held the officer tightly by the arms, and that it was as he was being restrained in this manner that he had undoubtedly been shot by a third man. At the conclusion of the evidence, the three accused were committed to stand trial for wilful murder at the next assizes, and this was also the finding when they appeared before the magistrates.

Constable Byrne was a native of County Down, who had served in the Cumberland Constabulary for twelve years. Before being posted to Plumpton, he had served at Alston and was a highly respected officer, both by colleagues and the residents of the communities he had served. He left a widow and four children, the youngest being just one month old.

His funeral took place on Sunday 1 November, and a detachment of police officers marched in front of the hearse on its journey from the Pack Horse to Penrith cemetery, where 3,000 mourners heard Father Meynell conduct the burial service and praise the dead officer for his courage and devotion to duty.

The trial of Baker, Rudge and Martin opened on Monday 18 January 1886 at Carlisle Assizes, before Mr Justice Day, and lasted for three days. Mr Littler QC, who led for the Crown, was assisted by Mr Shee and Mr Fell. Rudge and Martin were represented by Mr Cavanagh. Baker, who was clearly attempting to distance himself from his co-defendants, was represented by Mr Mattinson and Mr Lumb. The three accused pleaded not guilty to the murder of Constable Byrne.

Interestingly, John Plenderleith, the valet at Netherby Hall, had reported seeing several sets of finger marks on the window through which the burglars had gained entry to Lady Hermione's bedroom, but the significance of fingerprints in solving crimes had not yet been recognised, and of course they were not then used as evidence. However, the Crown had a strong case, and although the jury was only to determine the guilt or otherwise of the accused for murder, Mr Littler and his team provided witnesses to all of their alleged crimes. They reasoned that when viewed as a whole, there was a compelling chain of evidence against the men in the dock.

Following the arrests of Rudge and Martin at Tebay station, a search had been made of the surrounding area, and on the bank of the River Lune an eardrop was found, which Lady Hermione identified as one of the stolen items. It was surmised that the men had decided to throw the stolen jewellery into the river, for if they were found with it in their possession it would have been extremely incriminating. The eardrop must have fallen short and it was decided to make a search of the river. Constable Thomas Scott was ordered to undertake this, and after eight days his perseverance paid off. He found a tobacco pouch containing the rest of the missing jewellery, including the matching eardrop.

Constable Byrne. (Illustrated Police News)

The defence could of course have argued that this was simply circumstantial, but corroborative evidence was offered. After the accused men had been placed in Carlisle Gaol, the governor, Joseph Leavers, was concerned that Baker might attempt to take his own life. To prevent this, he arranged for two prisoners, Robert Cummings and John Baker, to share a cell with him. Baker subsequently told his cellmates that Rudge and Martin had assured him that they had disposed of the jewellery by throwing it into the river. When the prisoners gave their evidence at the trial, the defence attempted to discredit them by suggesting they had lied to gain favourable treatment in the gaol. However, this was shown to be unlikely as both were short-term prisoners with nothing to gain by attending the trial and giving their evidence.

Witnesses were called who could link the men to all of the relevant crime scenes, and when they attempted to escape from the district. Their suitcases were produced in court and their contents showed them to be quite simply burglary kits. Other vital evidence was provided by their revolvers, which could have been used to kill the constable and wound the others, and blood was found on the coats of all three men.

Mr Cavanagh argued that there was no evidence to suggest that his clients, Rudge and Martin, had participated in the Netherby Hall burglary. He claimed the crime had been committed by a fourth man, whose identity was not known, who later handed the jewels to his clients for safe keeping, which they admitted. This would explain how they came to have them at Tebay, where they attempted to throw them into the river, so they would not be found in possession of them. At the time the fatal shot was heard throughout Plumpton, his clients were said to be still in the Pack Horse. He acknowledged that after leaving the inn they encountered the fourth man in the road standing over the dying constable. He also accepted that they had helped him throw the constable over the wall into the field. He concluded by suggesting they should not be facing a murder charge but one of being accessories after the fact.

Mr Mattison argued that Baker, unlike his two co-defendants was never in possession of a revolver, and as nobody had witnessed the shooting of Constable Byrne, it could not be proven that he had participated in the crime. The murder might have been committed by one or both of the other men in the dock, or by someone else. It was not for him to prove who had committed the murder, and his task was limited to demonstrating that his client had not been responsible. He believed he had shown the jury that his client was innocent of murder, and that Baker should therefore be found not guilty.

The jury retired at a few minutes past eight in the evening and returned one hour later, having found all three guilty of the murder of Constable Byrne. When asked if they had anything to say, the prisoners claimed they were innocent, and continued to do so as they were taken down into the cells.

The trial having finished, the judge took the opportunity to praise the heroic conduct of the police officers, Roche, Johnstone and Fortune. He singled out Constable Byrne, who knowing what he did of the armed men, did not hesitate to confront them alone and without a weapon. The judge also highlighted the heroism of the railwaymen who, despite being unarmed, had played such a vital role in the arrest of the three murderers. The judge ordered that £177 from public funds should be shared between the brave public servants and Mrs Byrne.

Carlisle Town Council opened a public appeal to help Mrs Byrne and also to recognise the courage of the police officers who had been wounded, and the gallant railwaymen. Donations were received from all parts of the country, especially from police officers. For instance, a collection among members of the Birmingham force raised £9, and Cumberland-born Leonard Henderson, the Deputy Chief Constable of West Sussex, sent half a sovereign. Sir Frederick Graham donated £50, and Lady Hermione visited Constable Byrne's widow to assure her that she and her husband would take an interest in her children's futures.

The rules of the Metropolitan and City Police Orphanage permitted entry only to the children of London officers. However, an anonymous donor offered a donation of £500 if this rule was relaxed and the Byrne children were allowed to enter. The committee agreed and the proposal was welcomed by Mrs Byrne. Although there would be periods of separation, this would ensure that all of her children would receive an excellent education. A child had to be between seven and twelve years of age to be admitted, so her eldest son could enter immediately, and the other children would follow in later years.

It was arranged that the executions would take place on Monday 8 February 1886 at Carlisle Gaol, and the three condemned men were to be hanged simultaneously. A new gallows was constructed in the old treadmill shed, comprising a lengthy cross beam, to which three iron rings were fixed, through which the ropes would be suspended. James Berry was given the task, and although he was very experienced, and had officiated at six double hangings, this would be his first triple execution. It was arranged therefore that he would be assisted by Charles Maldon.

The condemned men received a number of family visits, and Rudge spent much of his time writing on the conditions in convict prisons, which he asked be sent to the Prison Commissioners after his death. The press reported that Martin continued to deny any involvement in the Romford murder, but in the early hours of the morning of his execution, he had confessed that it was he who had shot Constable Byrne, and Rudge and Baker had held Byrne by his arms as he did so. Later, James Berry revealed that as he prepared him for his execution, Martin told him that it was he who had shot Inspector Simmons.

At the trial, Baker had decided on his own defence strategy, which led to him distancing himself from the other two men. He had also provided the authorities with information, which presumably he hoped would help his case. For instance he reported that after Constable Fortune had been knocked unconscious, and fearing he might die, Rudge and Martin had placed him on the railway track, so that when hit by a train it would look like an accident. Much to the annoyance of the other two men, Baker had returned and lifted the constable off the line and put him in a safe place. His parents tried desperately to have his sentence commuted to one of life imprisonment, arguing that he had not had a gun and had not fired the fatal shot. They also attempted to suggest that he had been under the influence of two more experienced and dangerous criminals. However, their son would not be reprieved.

In the days leading up to their executions, the condemned men helped clear up the mystery of the fourth man. They refused to name him but said he was a criminal known to Baker, whom they met by chance on their arrival in the district. He advised them that he intended walking to Carlisle on Wednesday evening, so they arranged to meet him after the Netherby Hall burglary, of which he knew nothing, so they could make the journey together. He was with them at the time of the shootings in Kingstown and when they confronted Hadley. However, he took no part and remonstrated with them before hastily taking his leave. There was no significant attempt to trace the man, whose identity was never discovered.

On the morning of the executions the three men met briefly before entering the shed, and were able to say their goodbyes to each other and shake hands. Their names had been written in chalk on the drop so each man knew where to stand, and they died without incident. Following the inquest they were buried within the walls of the prison.

It emerged later that James Berry's assistant, Charles Maldon, was in fact Sir Claude Champion De Crespigny, a well-known entrepreneur and sportsman. There was a public outcry that an amateur hangman was allowed to assist at an execution, but Sir Claude argued that at some future date he anticipated being invited to become a County Sheriff, and he would therefore be required to organise and witness executions. It was not, he insisted, in his nature to require anyone to perform any task he was unable or unwilling to perform himself. He had therefore obtained the permission of the High Sheriff of Cumberland to assist at the executions, subject to James Berry's agreement. The executioner raised no objections after Sir Claude agreed to pay Berry £5 for the privilege of assisting him.

EIGHT

A SHOOTING AT THE BARRACKS

⭄ BARROW, 1917 ⭆

It was almost three thirty in the afternoon on Saturday 13 January 1917, and Captain Webb, the officer in command of B Company of the Royal Welsh Fusiliers, based in the Cavendish Dock Barracks at Barrow, was sitting in his office. Suddenly the silence was shattered by what he immediately recognised to be the sound of a rifle shot. It came from the direction of the orderly room, which was about 30 yards away. The Captain ran to the scene to find Sergeant Major Henry Lynch on the floor, conscious but obviously in great pain with blood pouring from a throat wound.

Captain Webb was informed that Private Thomas Clinton was responsible for shooting the Sergeant Major, and that he had already been detained and taken to the guard room. The Captain saw Clinton's rifle leaning against the wall, and gave instructions that nobody should touch it, before arranging for the town's civilian police to be made aware of the incident. Dr George Alexander was in the barracks' hospital and, having heard the shot, reached the scene within minutes. He found the Sergeant Major still breathing, but the wound was so serious that there was nothing he could do for the man, who died a few minutes later.

Detective Inspector Duckworth arrived at the barracks, and following his preliminary enquiries, Clinton was arrested and taken to the local police station. It did not take the Inspector long to reconstruct the events of earlier that afternoon. He took a statement from Sergeant Joe Barrow, who had been in charge of the guard that day. He explained that the guard comprised fourteen men, including Private Clinton, who were on duty for a twenty-four hour period. Each spent two hours on sentry duty, after which they were stood down for two hours. Clinton was in the third relief and was not due to take up his post until seven o'clock that evening. He was not permitted to leave the guard room before then, and he was certainly not allowed to take his rifle out of the room. On reporting for duty, each man was issued with a rifle, bayonet, and twenty cartridges, fifteen of which were placed in his pouch and the remaining five loaded into the magazine. When asked by the Inspector if he had noticed anything unusual about Clinton's behaviour that day, the Sergeant replied that when he first reported for duty, Clinton had complained bitterly that he had not been provided with a dinner. On hearing the shot, the Sergeant had turned out the guard, and it was only then that he realised that Clinton and his weapon were missing. The Private had left the guard room without permission, taking the loaded rifle with him.

The Inspector next interviewed Lance Corporal William Davies, one of the two men, other than the deceased, who were in the orderly room at the time of the shooting. Davies stated that he had been standing close to the stove, which was about 6ft away from the door. The Sergeant Major was sitting at his desk when Clinton entered the room with his rifle in the on-guard position, and which was pointing directly at the deceased. Clinton shouted, 'Now then, Sergeant Major', which was followed immediately by a shot. The victim put his hands to his throat, and as he fell from his chair he cried out, 'I am dead! I am dead!'

Clinton left the room and the Lance Corporal saw him throw down his weapon, walk out of the building and collapse to the ground on his knees, with his hands covering his face. As members of the guard arrived, the Lance Corporal explained to them what had occurred, and they led Clinton to the guardroom.

Private William Smithers was also in the orderly room, and was standing close to the door when Clinton appeared and addressed the Sergeant Major, which was followed by the shot. Private Smithers was so distressed at the events he witnessed that he fainted and was unaware of what happened immediately following the shooting.

The Royal Welsh Fusiliers provided security for the docks at Barrow. (Author's collection)

I am an Architect practising at Barrow-in-Furness.

I have prepared and produce:-

1. Block Plan shewing site and offices referred to by witnesses in this case and their location as to surrounding Docks and Buildings.

2. Plan shewing:-

Guard Room. 30' 9" long. 15' 10" wide. The position of the Arms rack will be seen at right hand side of entrance.

Company Office. Distant from Guardroom 19' 7". This office is 24' long and 8' 6" wide. Height 7' 5" to eaves. The window in the Company Office coming from Guard Room which Prisoner would pass is distant 3' 6" from the corner of the Company Office is glass space of 1' 9" wide and 2' $7\frac{1}{2}$" high from the ground to the bottom of the window is 3' $10\frac{1}{2}$".

I have also shewn the height of window's base the cross bar of window is 1' 7" high. Anyone passing the window could if he desired clearly see anyone seated at the table. The window is clear sheet glass.

The door is 10' 9" from the corner of the building and 5' 5" from the windows. The door is hung on the nearest side to the Guard Room and opens outwards. The door is 2' 9" wide.

In the interior of the Company's Office turning to the right on entering is a table 5' 11" long, 2' 6" wide. The distance from the doorway to this table at its nearest point is 1' 2" and to the form on which deceased was sitting about 5'

From this table to the one at which witness was sitting is 5' 9". Directly opposite the doorway is a stove distant about $6\frac{1}{2}$'.

Orderly Room. Coloured blue on plan is 5' 7" from the line of rail and is 31' from the Company Office.

Capt: Webb's Room. At the back of the Orderly Room and distant therefrom 14' 10" is Capt: Webb's room and this is distant from the Company Office 65'.

Sentry Boxes. One is 2' from the Guard Room and at the back thereof.

The other is opposite the Company Office and distant therefrom 26'

The plans and particulars shewn thereon including measurements have all been taken by me and are correct.

Details of the plans of the buildings in the barracks, provided by local architect Edward Muir Young. (National Archives)

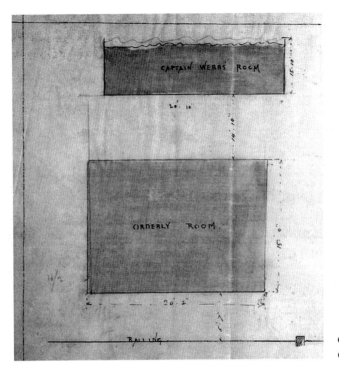

Captain Webb's office and the Orderly Room. (National Archives)

Upon his arrival at the police station, Clinton, a twenty-eight-year-old Mancunian who had enlisted in 1915, was initially charged with attempted murder, as it had not been confirmed that his victim was dead. The prisoner made the following statement to Detective Inspector Duckworth: 'Will you answer me the question? Did the bullet strike him? That's what I want to know. He has been a scamp to everybody in the company. I am sorry to say he has been a bad'un.'

Shortly afterwards, Clinton, who was unaware that the Sergeant Major had died, called out from his cell to Constable Townson, 'Did the bullet go near the Sergeant Major? It is a pity it did not kill him, he is a bastard!' Later, when Constable Good was in the cell area, Clinton asked, 'Did the bullet strike the Sergeant Major?' The constable replied that he did not know and Clinton continued, 'He is a swine; it is a wonder he has not been laid out before. I was as near to him as I am to you, and I let go at him. He deserved all he got.'

Later that evening, when it was confirmed that his victim had died, Clinton was charged with his murder. There appeared to be no immediately obvious motive for the crime, but it seemed to the Inspector that the prisoner's feelings of resentment towards the non-commissioned officer had intensified over a period of several weeks. He learnt that on 4 November 1916, when the regiment was in Bebbington, Sergeant Major Lynch had reported Clinton to his superiors for being drunk when he reported for guard duty. He later gave evidence against him which led to Clinton being sentenced to seven days custody, and receiving a fine of 7s 6d. It was possible that not having had his dinner on the day of the shooting was the issue that had tipped Clinton over the edge, and his rage was irrationally directed towards Sergeant Major Lynch.

On the morning of 15 January there was a brief hearing in the local magistrates' court, when the police asked for an adjournment of eight days. After remanding Clinton to Preston Gaol, the bench agreed to a request from Major Maples, the Garrison Staff Officer, to make a brief statement on behalf of the regiment. He began by stating that the deceased, a native of Cork, was thirty-nine years old, and his wife and children were living locally. He had served with the regiment for almost twenty-two years, and his death was very much regretted by his comrades. The Major described an excellent non-commissioned officer who had always performed his duties to the very highest of standards.

The inquest started during the afternoon of 15 January, before the coroner, F.W. Poole. Chief Constable John Berry spoke on behalf of the police but Clinton was not represented. At the request of the coroner, a senior army officer who was not directly involved in the case agreed to sit with Clinton, should he require assistance during the proceedings.

The police called Dr Alexander to provide medical evidence, along with the soldiers who had witnessed the events of the previous Saturday afternoon, and the police officers who had heard the statements made by the accused at the police station following his arrest. Prior to these witnesses being called to give their evidence, the coroner had advised Clinton that he was entitled to cross-examine any of the witnesses should he wish to do so. He did indeed question several of them, in particular Private Smithers and Constable Townson.

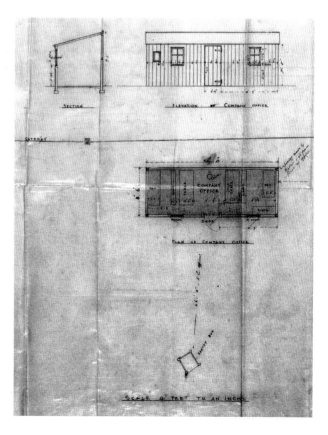

The Company Office.
(National Archives)

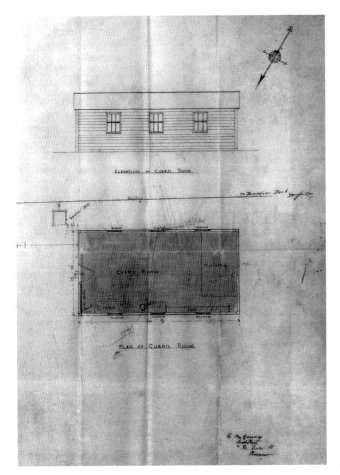

The Guard Room. (National Archives)

Private Smithers had been the person closest to him when the fatal shot was fired, and he conceded under questioning by Clinton that he had not actually seen the trigger being pulled. Clinton was attempting to establish that the shooting had been accidental, which was to form the basis of his defence. He also denied making the derogatory remarks about the dead man, which implied that he believed the dead man had received his just desserts. As the following exchange demonstrates, he accused Constable Townson of lying:

Clinton: Are you sure I called him a bastard?
Townson: Yes.
Clinton: You swear I called him a bastard? I might have said something about a bullet, but I never called him that name.
Coroner (to Townson): You have no doubt about it?
Townson: No doubt at all.
Coroner: You wrote it down at the time?
Townson: Yes.
Clinton: You might have written it down but it is not true.

In his address to the jury, the coroner said, 'Whatever reason Clinton had for committing this act, there was no doubt, there could be no doubt, that he did it intentionally. There was no question of any accident. You can only bring in a verdict of murder.'

The jury rejected the accused man's claim that this had been an accidental shooting, and agreed with the coroner, for after a brief adjournment they returned with a verdict of wilful murder.

Eight days later, at the resumed hearing before the magistrates, Clinton persisted with his claim that the shooting had not been a deliberate act, and made the following statement from the dock, which was the only occasion his version of events was heard from his own lips:

On 13 January I was warned by the orderly sergeant to mount guard at two thirty. I fell in with the new guard by the huts and marched to Cavendish Dock. I had a complaint to make to the orderly officer. After he had inspected the guard I motioned to the orderly sergeant to tell him I wanted to speak to him. I told him that I had had no dinner, and he told the orderly sergeant he would see about getting me a dinner. The new guard was then marched off to the Cavendish guard room. The sergeant in charge was Sergeant Barrow. The old guard was dismissed and they handed over the rifles to the new guard. We then went into the guardroom and took off our water bottles and haversacks. We were given twenty rounds of ammunition by Sergeant Barrow. I loaded my rifle, putting five rounds in the magazine. Without thinking of what I did I went to the company office to see Sergeant Major Lynch over having no dinner. I said, 'Now, Sergeant Major.' He was writing. He looked up from his paper and gave me a terrible look. Before I knew what happened, the rifle went off. I was confused at the time. If I had any spite against him, if I had ever meant to do him harm, I could have done so many a time when I was on number two post at Cavendish Dock. He was going backwards and forwards to the sergeant's mess at all hours. If I had wished him any harm I could have done it whilst on sentry duty. All I have got to say now is people in Barrow won't look upon me as a murderer when they know the truth. They will understand things. The lads in the camp will also do. I do not think I have one enemy in the whole camp.

At the conclusion of the hearing, Clinton was committed to stand trial at the next Manchester Assizes, which took place on 15 February before trial judge Mr Justice Shearman. A.H. Maxwell and Lindon Riley prosecuted, and Clinton was represented by Gilbert Jordan.

As had been anticipated, the issue to be decided by the jury was whether the shooting had been an accident or a deliberate act. The compelling prosecution evidence, which had been presented at the earlier hearings, was again given. Mr Jordan, however, argued that the death of Sergeant Major Lynch had not been planned by his client, whose behaviour before and after the shooting was consistent with his explanation that it had been an accident.

The judge's summing up to the jury was very fair, and he told them it was for them alone to decide between the two distinct versions of events that they had been presented with during the trial. There were, he continued, only two verdicts open to them: not guilty if they believed the defendant, and guilty of murder if they accepted the Crown's evidence.

The jury found Clinton guilty of murder, and when asked if he had anything to say before sentence was passed, he replied, 'I have one thing to say. Although these gentlemen have found me guilty, there is one, the Great Judge of All, who knows I am innocent.'

In passing the death sentence, the judge made it clear that he agreed wholeheartedly with the jury's decision. There was to be no reprieve, and Clinton was hanged by John Ellis at Strangeways Gaol, Manchester on 21 March 1917. In the past, some serving military men had been granted permission to be hanged in their uniform, but Clinton's request that he be executed and later buried in his army uniform was refused, as it was considered he had brought disgrace to his regiment.

NINE

MURDER FOR GAIN

⚜ BARROW, 1942 ⚜

Thomas Clinton was hanged for a crime committed during the First World War, and another murder occurred in Barrow twenty-five years later, as war raged across Europe yet again.

Thirty-nine-year-old Nellie Pearson lived at 85 Undergreens Road, Hawcoat with her husband John, a joiner, her seventeen-year-old daughter Joyce and her eighty-six-year-old mother. The family had moved to this address a few months earlier after their previous home, at No. 12 on the same road, had been destroyed by enemy bombing in the spring blitz of the previous year. For the previous fifteen years Nellie, a popular, cheerful woman, who was known to be devoted to her family, had worked as a collector for the Midland Clothing Company. The job involved calling on local residents who had purchased clothes, which were to be paid for by weekly instalments.

She loved her work, and being a local woman, she had known a number of her customers all her life, and some had been her close personal friends for many years. She kept to a similar routine every day so all of her customers knew when to expect her, and on Monday 5 October 1942 at four thirty in the afternoon, she called on Helen Robertshaw, with whom she had gone to school, at her home at 2E Steamer Street. As usual, the two old friends spent a few minutes chatting, and having said goodbye, Nellie set off to her next call, but she would not be seen alive again.

The failure of Nellie to return home at the usual time that day led to her husband very quickly experiencing a sense of unease. He retraced her route for that day, but could find no sign of her, and reported her missing to the police. They too retraced her movements, and extended their search over a wider area, including the Walney Channel in case she had drowned. Her relatives in various parts of the country were contacted, but nobody had seen or heard from her. As the police search continued into a third day, John confided to friends that he feared the worse, as he knew his wife would not voluntarily absent herself from her family.

Barrow, the setting for a brutal robbery and murder during the Second World War. (Author's collection)

WALNEY PROMENADE & CHANNEL, BARROW-IN-FURNESS.

The Walney Channel was searched after Nellie Pearson went missing. (Author's collection)

Having left Steamer Street, Nellie was next due to call at the top-floor flat of Catherine Worrall at 2G Brig Street. Mrs Worrall was separated from her husband and lived there with her seventeen-year-old son, Jack, and twenty-eight-year-old Ronald Roberts, who had lodged with her for two years. Mrs Worrall and her son each had a bedroom, and their lodger slept in the living room. He usually slept on the floor but more recently he had tried to use a camp bed. However, he had suffered from severely ulcerated legs since childhood, and he had found the bed uncomfortable and impossible to sleep on. In early September he decided to stop using it and it was folded up and placed in a recess in Mrs Worrall's bedroom.

The three of them pooled their wages, and household expenses were paid from this money. However, the lodger's legs had been causing him severe discomfort for a number of weeks, which had prevented him from reporting for work at the Vickers shipyard, where he was employed as an air-raid warden. At the time that Nellie was due to call, Roberts would have been alone in the flat. Police enquires had revealed that due to his lack of regular wages he had not been paying his way at the flat, and there were other indications that he had been experiencing financial difficulties. However, in the days following Nellie's disappearance he had started settling many of his debts. The suspicions of the investigating police team were therefore now focused on Ronald Roberts.

At 9.25 p.m. on the Thursday following Nellie's disappearance, Detective Chief Inspector Thompson and Inspector Cotton visited 2G Brig Street, and found Mrs Worrall and her lodger at home. The officers lost no time in confronting Roberts with their suspicions, stating that they believed he had been involved in the missing woman's disappearance.

Roberts denied having any knowledge of the mystery, and insisted, 'I never saw her. I was at the pictures.' Nevertheless, Chief Inspector Thompson continued by saying to him, 'I believe you were here near the time Mrs Pearson was here. Did you leave the pictures early?' Roberts replied that he had done so at 4.20 p.m., but he persisted in claiming he had not seen the missing woman that afternoon.

The officers were not satisfied, and with Mrs Worrall's agreement began to search the flat, which, because of the blackout regulations, had to be conducted by torchlight. The Chief Inspector entered Mrs Worrall's bedroom and after a few minutes moved the camp bed in the recess. Behind it he saw the body of a woman, and immediately recognised it as being that of Nellie Pearson, who he had known for many years. He shouted to his colleague, 'Grab him!'

Inspector Cotton did so, and a distressed Mrs Worrall ran from the room in tears. The officers searched Roberts and found a 10s note, 5s 6d in silver coins, and 11d in copper. Roberts whispered to the officers, 'I will tell you all about it,' but seemed reluctant to talk at the flat, apparently fearing that Mrs Worrall might be upset further. The officers took their prisoner to the central police station, where he made the following confession to Detective Thompson:

How it was, she came to our house and Mrs Worrall asked me to pay. I put a 10 shilling note on the table, and as she was getting the change I saw all the money, and after that I don't seem to remember anything. Before I realised what I had done, the worst had happened. I was frightened and I hid some of the money and the bag in the boiler of the back kitchen, and burned some of the money in the kitchen. I don't really remember what I did altogether.

Woman Club Collector's Body Found

AFTER a search lasting three days, Barrow-in-Furness police last night found the body of Mrs Nellie Pearson (37), a club collector, of Undergreens Road, Barrow, who had been missing since Monday, when she went on her rounds collecting

The body was found in a tenement House in Brig-street, Barrow Island, and a Home Office pathologist has been called in to examine it.

It was thought at first that Mrs Pearson was suffering from loss of memory and inquiries were made in various parts of the country for relatives.

A man had been questioned about the woman's disappearance.

A newspaper report of the discovery of the body.
(Author's collection)

The police were convinced that Roberts had acted alone, and that Mrs Worrall had been unaware that for three nights she had shared her bedroom with a corpse, which had been concealed only a few feet away from her bed. She advised the police that in the days following the disappearance, her lodger had cleaned and disinfected the flat several times, but as he had done so in the past when she and her son were at work, she had not found this suspicious.

In the hours that followed, investigators retrieved important pieces of evidence from the flat, and following the preliminary findings of the Forensic Science Laboratory at Preston, and the post-mortem performed on Tuesday afternoon, Roberts was charged with Nellie's murder at twenty past six the following evening.

The accused made a brief appearance before Councillor Mrs E.A. Ward, who sat alone as a magistrate on Saturday morning. She agreed to a police request to remand him in custody until 30 October so that they might complete their enquiries. The inquest opened almost immediately before Deputy Coroner J. Poole. Following formal identification of the deceased by Detective Thompson, Mr Poole issued a burial certificate and adjourned the inquest *sine die*.

Nellie was buried on the afternoon of the following Tuesday in St Matthew's Church cemetery. There were sixty-five wreaths from family, friends and customers, together with a floral tribute from Barrow Owner Occupiers' Association, and her husband's workmates at the joiners' shop at Vickers Armstrong.

By the time of the adjourned appearance before the magistrates, the police had completed their enquiries. Several incriminating articles were discovered in the kitchen boiler at the flat, despite the accused's attempt to burn them. They found her handbag, part of her dress, a towel, a pair of man's trousers and braces, a white shirt and blue overalls, all of which were stained with blood. There were also five food ration books belonging to the Pearson family. A piece of red fabric was found hidden under some coal, which John Pearson recognised as being from the turban his wife had been wearing on the day of her disappearance. Also discovered in the flat were a £1 note and a 10s note, both of which were bloodstained.

The Director of the Forensic Science Laboratory at Preston, J.B. Firth informed the magistrates that Nellie's blood group was A, in common with forty per cent of the population. Group A was found on most of the items recovered at the flat, although he was unable to confirm the group of the blood found on the notes and on the hammer. However, he found human hair similar to that of the murdered woman on the hammer and on the man's trousers, which, from their condition, he believed had been used to clean the scene after the crime had been committed. He also found group A blood on the penknife.

The post-mortem was performed by the local police surgeon, Dr Francis Carson of Abbey Road, Barrow, who concluded that Nellie had been dead for between two and three days when the body was discovered. There was evidence of five heavy blows to the head, one of which had caused a skull fracture. There was also a large bruise on her forehead, and these injuries had led to bleeding in the skull. There were three wounds to the neck, one of which had perforated the windpipe and which had been caused by a sharp instrument. He believed these had been inflicted several hours after the head injuries, whilst she was still alive.

He conceded that the bruise on the forehead could possibly have been sustained due to an accidental fall, but this could not be said of any of the other injuries. She had slowly bled to death over a period of several hours. Her death had been prolonged and painful, and from the additional information provided by Mr Firth, he was certain that after the injuries had been caused initially to the head with the hammer, the penknife had been used later to inflict the neck wounds in order to finish her off.

When the body was discovered it was noted that several items of her clothing had been removed, and some of her underclothes and blouse had been pulled up to her neck. This suggested a possible sexual element to the crime, but this was not pursued as the police were convinced that the prime motive had been financial gain. Nellie's husband told the detectives that when he last saw her on the Monday morning at seven o'clock, his wife had more than £20 in notes and silver in her handbag. When she disappeared she was near to the end of that day's round so she would have been in possession of considerably more cash.

The police discovered that their suspect had not paid any money towards the household expenses for some weeks, and that he was heavily in debt to a number of people. However, within a short time of Nellie's disappearance, he settled many of these, and he had also spent a considerable sum of money on a number of individuals.

Ronald Roberts worked as an air-raid warden at Vickers. (Author's collection)

Furthermore, the police found several individuals who revealed that in the days before the crime, their prisoner had told them that he was due to receive some money on the Monday, and the investigating officers had been able to establish that the different explanations that he gave were untrue. He told some that he had won eight guineas on the pools, but Harry Bailey of Unity Pools confirmed that although he had submitted a coupon for the first time on 26 September, he had not won any money. Roberts told his neighbour, Joseph Pickering, that he was a Dunkirk veteran and had been receiving a navy pension but due to an administrative error this had not been paid for several weeks. However, the problem had now been resolved, and he would soon be receiving a large cheque for the arrears he was owed. The police were able to establish that he had not been at Dunkirk, and was not entitled to draw a pension of any description.

In early 1942, Roberts was elected treasurer of a tontine group, which had been formed by the air-raid wardens at Vickers Armstrong. By July their combined weekly contributions totalled £20 11s, which Roberts claimed to have lost. He agreed to repay the full amount at the rate of 25s each week, and by mid-September he had repaid £4 15s. However, he missed a payment at the end of the month, but assured his section officer, Edwin Remington that he would be able to pay this as soon as he had sold his piano accordion. Mr Remington advised the police that Roberts made a payment of £8 on the night of Nellie's disappearance. The police quickly discovered that Roberts had never possessed a piano accordion, and could not therefore have raised those funds by selling one.

Several people reported seeing Roberts with relatively large amounts of cash in the days between Nellie's disappearance and his arrest. On the Monday night, he took his landlady to the cinema, paid for a fish and chip supper, and afterwards took her for a drink. On the Wednesday night, he took Mrs Worrall to a dance and they later visited a number of local pubs, including the Royal and the Devonshire Hotel. At the Royal he met an old friend, Trooper Thomas Douglas, who was home on leave. Roberts handed him 10s, saying he wished to treat him to a few drinks. Margaret Copeland reported a visit to her home by Roberts on the Tuesday, when he gave her 12s, which he asked her to pass to her sister so she could buy a dress for her baby.

He also settled some of his debts, beginning with £8 in rent arrears. He also paid some outstanding bills owing to local shopkeepers, which included 12s to grocer Joseph Hill on Steamer Road, and £1 2d to newsagent Annie McAleese on Island Road. He paid £2 4s 3d to grocer Harry O'Hare on Ramsden Dock Road; and 15s to Margaret Burrows, who managed a battery charging shop on Schooner Street. Roberts also redeemed a suit and ring he had previously pawned with Tooner and Dennisons by paying £1 9s 6d for those two items, together with an additional 5s for a pair of second-hand shoes.

He was committed to stand trial at the Manchester Assizes, and was granted legal representation under the Poor Persons Act. The trial began on Wednesday 9 December before Mr Justice Stable, and lasted three days. The case for the Crown was conducted by Justin Lynskey KC and A.E. Jalland, and the defence was led by Edward Wooll.

The prosecution relied largely on the evidence already given before the magistrates, but to support their theory that this was a premeditated crime, evidence was produced that Roberts had told some of those to whom he owed money that he was due to receive a large amount of money on Monday 28 September. This was the week before the murder, when Nellie had been due to call at 2G Brig Street. However, on that day Mrs Worrall arrived home early and met Nellie on the stairs leading to the flat. She handed her that week's payment, and Nellie did not therefore have to call at the flat where Roberts was waiting for her. If she had done so, the prosecution claimed that she would have died at his hands a week earlier.

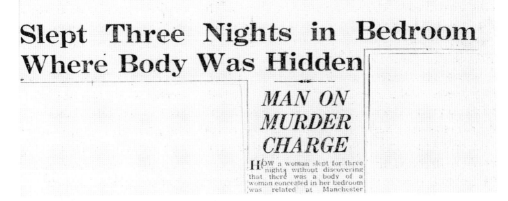

Slept Three Nights in Bedroom Where Body Was Hidden

MAN ON MURDER CHARGE

How a woman slept for three nights without discovering that there was a body of a woman concealed in her bedroom was related at Manchester

A newspaper account of the trial. (Author's collection)

Manchester Assizes. (Author's collection)

The defence called no witnesses and Roberts did not take the stand. In his closing speech to the jury, Mr Wooll acknowledged that there was an element of premeditation, but he argued that his client had not been in his right mind at the time of the killing. For instance, there was no plan for disposing of the body, or any attempt at escape. He suggested that these were not the actions of a man thinking rationally, and he should be convicted of committing murder when insane. This argument was firmly rejected by Mr Justice Stable, who in his closing summary emphasised that no evidence had been provided to support the theory that the accused had been insane at the time the murder had occurred, which the law demanded. The jury obviously agreed with the judge, for after retiring for just fifteen minutes they returned with a verdict of wilful murder.

There was little support for a reprieve, and Roberts was executed at Liverpool's Walton Gaol on Wednesday 10 February 1943 by Thomas Pierrepoint, who was assisted by Harry Kirk.

BIBLIOGRAPHY

PAMPHLETTS

Woodward, C., *A Correct and Full Account of the Trial of Mr John Hatfield, Who Married the Beauty of Buttermere and Who was Convicted of Foraery at Carlisle Assizes on Monday August 15 1803* (Liverpool, 1803)

NEWSPAPERS

Barrow Times
Cumberland and Westmoreland Advertiser
Cumberland Paquet
East Cumberland News
Guardian (Barrow)
Illustrated Police News
Liverpool Daily Courier
Liverpool Mercury
Manchester Evening News
North Western Evening Mail
Penrith Herald
Penrith Observer

Other local titles published by The History Press

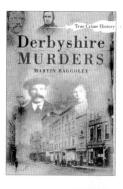

Derbyshire Murders
MARTIN BAGGOLEY

Derbyshire Murders brings together ten of the county's most extraordinary and shocking cases. The crimes covered made not just local but in some cases national headlines. For this fascinating, illustrated collection, Martin Baggoley has returned to original sources – including police interviews, trial transcripts and contemporary newspaper reports – to rebuild each story from scratch.

978 0 7509 4507 3

Murder & Crime: Lancashire
MARTIN BAGGOLEY

This collection of local tales and murder cases from across the county of Lancashire is illustrated with more than sixty archive photographs, reward notices and drawings from the *Illustrated Police News*. With in-depth chapters recounting true cases of theft, violence, villainy and murder covering more than a century of criminal history, this chilling catalogue of murderous misdeeds is sure to horrify and captivate anyone interested in the criminal history of the area.

978 0 7524 4358 4

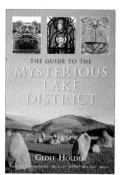

The Guide to the Mysterious Lake District
GEOFF HOLDER

This is the guide to everything strange, mysterious and uncanny that has occurred in the beautiful and rugged Lake District. Every historic site and ancient monument is explored – including stone circles, ancient cairns and crumbling stations – along with the many hidden treasures to be found in the area. From the strange histories of the Romantic poets to modern sightings of ghosts, UFOs and monsters in the lakes, it is an indispensable companion for the traveller about to travel into the mysterious realms of the Lake District.

978 0 7524 4987 6

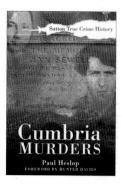

Cumbria Murders
PAUL HESLOP

Cumbria Murders brings together numerous murderous tales that shocked not only the county but also made headlines throughout the country. They include the cases of Wai Sheung Siu Miao, strangled while on honeymoon in 1928; William Armstrong, shot by the Revd Joseph Smith in 1851; Ann Sewell, stabbed to death by farmhand George Cass in 1860; and the murder of Jack West at his home near Workington in 1964, whose killers were the last two men to be lawfully hanged in England.

978 0 7509 4748 0

Visit our website and discover thousands of other History Press books.

www.thehistorypress.co.uk